Value in a Digital World

Francisco J. López Lubián • José Esteves

Value in a Digital World

How to assess business models and measure value
in a digital world

Francisco J. López Lubián
IE Business School. IE University
Madrid, Spain

José Esteves
IE Business School. IE University
Madrid, Spain

ISBN 978-3-319-84732-0   ISBN 978-3-319-51750-6 (eBook)
DOI 10.1007/978-3-319-51750-6

Cover illustration: Getty image/ildogesto

Printed on acid-free paper

This Palgrave Macmillan imprint is published by Springer Nature
The registered company is Springer International Publishing AG
The registered company address is: Gewerbestrasse 11, 6330 Cham, Switzerland

To our families

Preface

Valuation matters.

Not valuation as a pure academic exercise, but valuation as a business process in which we want to determine the reasonable worth of a company. Any reasonable value of any company depends on the future of that company. Since the future of many companies depends on how they deal with the digital world, valuation in a digital world is an interesting subject for many companies.

This is a book about the digital world and how to evaluate its importance in economic terms.

Digital technologies are reshaping our individual, social and cultural lives in unprecedented ways. Their integration into everyday life has a range of consequences for individuals, families, communities, governments and organizations. Economies are restructured, social life is reconfigured, organizations are reorganized and knowledge is produced. A new type of economy – the digital economy – is emerging: an economic system based on digital technologies, where trade and investment are global and firms compete with knowledge, networking and agility on a global basis.

The fast development and adoption of new technologies such as social media, mobile, cloud, the Internet of Things, artificial intelligence or 3D printing is creating new human and business development opportunities. The digital revolution has reached a scale and level of impact that no business, industry or government can ignore. The future of countries, businesses and individuals will depend more than ever on whether they embrace digital technologies.

Consider this fact. A decade ago, the five most valuable companies on Standard & Poor's 500 Index were Exxon, GE, Microsoft, Gazprom and

Citigroup. Today, the ranking has radically changed. The index's top five most valuable companies are in tech: Apple, Alphabet (parent company of Google), Amazon, Microsoft and Facebook.

This is certainly a new time and place – one dominated increasingly by horizontal digital platforms, virtual networks and Big Data that span traditional industry verticals. And new companies such as Facebook, LinkedIn, Uber and Airbnb have sprung up to take advantage of today's new opportunities – to build horizontal platforms that leverage the assets of you and me and what we have (cars and homes), do (drive) and know (friends).

On the other hand, it is well known that, in order to survive, any business – digital or not – needs to be economically sustainable. Economic sustainability implies that a business is economically feasible and profitable. It also implies the creation of economic value. And it is well known that, for any business, the normal way to create economic value is to invest in assets that generate it.

The purpose of this book is to discuss and explain how to select and manage digital assets or digital capabilities in order to create economic value.

This is not a book about digital transformation or about the steps needed to implement a digital transformation strategy. Neither is it a book about digital technologies.

As noted above, this is a book about the digital world. More specifically, it is about the importance of digital assets and capabilities in business, and how to evaluate this importance in economic terms. It's a book not about digital transformation, but about how to choose and manage digital assets and capabilities in a digital transformation process, in order to create economic value.

These days, every company either is or must become a digital organization if it wants to survive and grow in the age of platforms and networks. As a consequence, there has been a boom in acquisitions and restructuring in companies related to digital business. In some cases, one of the most controversial issues has been the rationality of the economic valuation of these operations, reflected in the final price. This book intends to shed some light on this topic.

Note that we do not deal with the special case of startup valuation. This is a very specific and important topic which needs individual treatment, probably in a book dedicated to the subject.

Since this book deals with the digital economy and economic value, Chapters 1 and 2 are dedicated to these topics, developing and discussing the basic concepts needed in order to understand them. For example, Chapter 1 includes discussions about the SMAC (social, mobiles, analytics and cloud) revolution, the new consumer, business digitization, web revenue models and the sharing economy. In Chapter 2 we define economic value, explain how to measure it and develop practical examples to apply these concepts to the digital world.

Chapters 3 and 4 include examples of valuation for different digital companies, such as WhatsApp, Twitter, Instagram, Square, Tuenti and LinkedIn, in different contexts, purposes and circumstances: as a target for a possible acquisition, for an initial public offering (IPO), buying a brand, buying data, buying a complementary business, etc.

Chapter 5 deals with managing to deliver economic value in a digital world, discussing the key points to be considered in order to reach that objective.

Chapter 6 offers a practical framework to evaluate economic value applicable to digital business.

Finally, in Chapter 7 we summarize the main conclusions.

Since this book aims to be a practical guide for corporate managers, entrepreneurs, digital officers, CFOs (chief financial officers), venture capitalists, consultants and people interested in evaluating digital assets and capabilities, its content is based on academic and business experience of several years, and its authors have to thank several people who contributed with comments, data and critical analysis.

Although the cooperation of these friends has been crucial for the interest of this book, any remaining mistakes are, of course, the authors' responsibility.

List of Key Concepts

Digital economy
Digital revolution
Business digitization
Digital capabilities
Digital economy
Innovation
Web business models
Disruptive Innovation
Merchant and brokerage models
Community models
Infomediary models
Affiliate models
Advertising models
Manufacturer's direct models
Subscription models
Utility models
Other models: Freemium
Sharing economy
Economic value
Real options
Value metrics
Capital structure
Terminal value
Mergers and acquisitions
Amazon
Google

Facebook
WhatsApp
Twitter
IPO
Ant Financial Services
LinkedIn
Tuenti
Lynda.com
Truven Health Analytic, Inc.
Microsoft
Big Data
Artificial Intelligence
Robotics
Internet of Things
Augmented and virtual reality
Revenues models
IBM
Instagram
Reasonable value
Value perception gap
Value to business stakeholders
IT investments
Business cannibalization
Unicorns
Valuation pitfalls
Price and relative value
Price and fundamental value
Monetization
Financing
Negotiation
Operational risks
Financial risks

Contents

About the Authors

Francisco J. López Lubián is Professor and Chief of the Finance Department at IE Business School. He combined his teaching career with an intense career in business as former financial analyst at Hewlett-Packard, controller for the Sarrió Group, financial director for Sarrió Tisú and general financial director for the Isolux Group.

In his own words, "My main focus of interest is to discover how to create economic value and orient decisions in order to achieve it." In this area he has published numerous books, research cases, teaching notes and academic papers in such journals as the *Case Research Journal, The Journal of Applied Corporate Finance, The Journal of Financial Education* and *The Business Case Journal*. His most recent book, published by Prentice Hall, was *The Corporate Guide to Corporate Restructuring* (2014). Professor López Lubián regularly contributes to leading newspapers and magazines, including the *Financial Times* and *Forbes India*.

López Lubián is an expert in financial valuation and analysis, and is visiting professor of the International MBA at Universidad Adolfo Ibáñez in Chile, the Master in Finance at Universidad San Andrés in Argentina and the Master in Finance in EAFIT (Colombia). He is a Doctor of Economics from Universidad Barcelona and holds an MBA from IESE. He undertook postdoctoral studies at Harvard Business School as a visiting scholar. Furthermore he is a member of the North American Case Research Association (NACRA), the Society of Case Research and member of the Board in the Financial Education Association, where he is Case Editor of the Journal of Financial Education and Advances in Financial Education.

José Esteves is Professor of the IT Department at IE Business School. When José Esteves talks about information systems it is with intensity and a passion that is founded not only in the technology itself but also in the human side of these systems. Focusing on areas such as knowledge management, the implementation of enterprise systems and, more recently, enterprise risk management, Professor Esteves believes it is the way people interact with information technology that will determine the success or failure of its implementation.

A wealth of experience in the corporate world underpins this belief. As an information systems analyst and consultant for companies such as Ciba-Geigy and Sonae Group and before joining the academic world, Prof Esteves focused on understanding how information systems interacted with business processes and human resources management.

Professor Esteves holds a PhD in Software – Information Systems, Universidad Politécnica de Catalunya, Barcelona, Spain. He is also Master in Information Systems, Universidade do Minho, Braga, Portugal, and he has a Diploma in Business Administration, minor in financial management, Instituto Superior de Tecnologia Empresarial, Porto, Portugal. Professor Esteves is also chair of eGovernment Software AG- Alianza Sumaq, which focuses on the analysis and understanding of eGovernment initiatives in Spain and Latin America.

List of Figures

List of Tables

1

The New Digital Economy

Introduction

The fast development and adoption of new information technology (IT) such as social media, mobile, cloud, the Internet of Things, artificial intelligence and 3D printing is creating new human and business development opportunities. The digital revolution has already reached a significant scale and level of impact that no business, industry or government can ignore. The future of countries, businesses and individuals will depend more than ever on whether and how they embrace digital technologies.

Business leaders are expecting dislocating change in their business sectors owing to the impacts of the digital revolution. They see a shift towards decentralized business structures, business operations and competition on a global scale, and more virtual working environments. The changes brought about by the Digital Age will continue to reshape and transform how we work, force us to rethink what the workplace is, and give us the option to work anywhere and any time. Technology is breaking down geographic, cultural and personal barriers in amazing new ways.

The Digital Revolution

Digital technology is evolving at a phenomenal rate, and reshaping our individual, social and business activities in unprecedented ways with tremendous consequences. The economy is being restructured, social life modified,

© The Author(s) 2017
F.J. López Lubián, J. Esteves, *Value in a Digital World*,
DOI 10.1007/978-3-319-51750-6_1

organizations redesigned and knowledge produced and shared in unprecedented ways. A new kind of economy – the digital economy – is coming to
the fore: an economic system that is based on digital technology, characterized by being more global than local, more sharing than exploitative and
more data driven than ever.

The term digital revolution refers to the shift from analogue and mechanical electronic technology to digital technology. Although it started in the
1950s with the development of transistors, it was not until the late 1970s,
with the adoption of digital computers, that its impact became evident. The
digital revolution also defines a new period in human history – the information and knowledge age.

However, the large-scale development and advancement of the digital
revolution occurred with the Internet and later with the World Wide
Web. Here is a short chronological timeline of the main milestones to
date:

1. 1947–1979 – The transistor, which was invented in 1947, paved the way
   for the development of advanced digital computers. This led to a communications revolution, and eventually to the creation of the World Wide
   Web.
2. 1980s – The personal computer became mainstream in the form of
   desktop machines. The first cellphone was also introduced during
   this decade. In 1983, Motorola released its first commercial mobile
   phone.
3. 1990s – Tim Berners-Lee invented the World Wide Web in 1989 and it
   became publicly available in 1992. Throughout the 1990s, the Internet
   proved to be one of the greatest communication advances of the century.
   By the end of the decade, the impact of the Internet on the everyday lives
   of many citizens had already occurred.
4. 2000s – Developing countries started to accelerate Internet and mobile
   access and adoption; globally the number of Internet users continued to
   grow exponentially, e-commerce started to boom and television began to
   switch from analogue to digital signals.
5. 2010 and beyond – The Internet reached 2 billion users in 2010 and
   3 billion users in 2014, and social media users grew significantly (e.g.
   Facebook passed 1.5 billion users). Once a luxury, mobile communication has also become crucial: around 70% of the world's population own a mobile phone, and around 70% will have smartphones by
   2020. In 2015, mobile Internet usage exceeded fixed/desktop
   Internet usage. Technology has become ubiquitous and the famous

mantra of "Everyone, Anytime, Anywhere" has started to become a reality.

The digital revolution continues to evolve – with cloud, social media and mobile technologies (e.g. wireless broadband and 3G and 4G technologies) improving and expanding Internet access and use around the globe. As Manuel Castells has noted,[1] this digital revolution has created a new kind of society that is defined with different terms: information society, knowledge society, network society.

According to Gartner, worldwide IT expenditure is projected to total $3.49 trillion in 2016, a decline of 0.5% over 2015's expenditure of $3.5 trillion. Garnet mentions that the decline is mainly because of currency fluctuations. As shown in Table 1.1, businesses allocated almost 50% of their IT expenditure to telecommunications services and a little more than a quarter to IT services. IT devices, data centers and software accounted for almost one third of the total.

While expenditure in the IT services market is forecasted to return to growth in 2016, the device market is showing signs of market saturation in significant markets and is projected to decline 3.7% in 2016. Device sales decline is taking place because of a combination of factors (e.g. customers not wanting to upgrade their existing devices and economic conditions), which are geography-specific.

The forecasted annual worldwide spending in telecom services is forecasted to dip by 2.0% in 2016 to $1.4 trillion. Economic downturns in relevant markets such as Brazil and Russia are affecting telecom service spending. Slowing growth in China's economy is also affecting consumer and business confidence and reducing spend in fixed voice telephony services.

Table 1.1 Worldwide IT spending forecast (billions of US dollars)

	2015 Spending	2016 Spending	2016 Growth (%)
Devices	650	626	−3.7
Data Center Systems	171	175	2.1
Software	308	321	4.2
IT Services	910	929	2.1
Communications Services	1,470	1,441	−2.0
Overall IT	3,509	3,492	−0.5

Source: Gartner: http://www.gartner.com/newsroom/id/3277517

---

[1] Castells, M. (1996). *The Information Age: Economy, Society and Culture Volume I: The Rise of the Network Society*. Oxford: Blackwell.

Regarding enterprise IT services, the situation in these same three major telecom markets (Brazil, China and Russia) is spurring a move toward consolidation among businesses and consequently decreasing telecom connections and spend. On the other hand, mobile data spending is expected to grow owing to new bandwidth pricing strategies, mobile app usage and 4G/LTE network deployment worldwide.

Technological advances in cloud computing, social media, analytical techniques, digital communications and enterprise systems are resulting in a redefinition of what work is and how and where we engage with it. These applications have an impact on the way people think, feel and interact, and remote working is not considered an exception anymore. "Anytime, anywhere, any device" is becoming the mainstream in our digitally enhanced environment.

In the last decade, owing to the global and rapid spread of digital technology, digital gained importance in global flows strategy. A recent study by McKinsey shows that before 2005 "cross-border digital flows were almost non-existent." Nowadays, they contribute more to global economic growth than traditional flows of goods. All flows together were worth $7.8 trillion in 2014, raising global gross domestic product (GDP) by 10% over the past ten years.[2] Data flows alone account for 36% ($2.8 trillion). It is expected that data flows will increase by another nine times over the next five years, because of the increased growth of Web searches, video downloads, e-commerce transactions and the Internet of Things.

Global digitization has transformed global services and flows by reducing transaction and distribution costs. Global flows are influenced by three main components of digitization: the development of digital goods and services; the integration of digital features into "analogue" goods and services; and the development of digital platforms for manufacturing, exchange and consumption. Compared with prior globalization phases, this new phase of globalization is knowledge-centric, rather than capital- or labor-centric. Furthermore, global digitization reduces entry barriers – anyone with an Internet connection can participate and change the old business rules. New global business avenues no longer need big seed capital to operate and compete globally. With the help of digital marketplaces such as eBay, Alibaba, Rakuten and Amazon, even small businesses and startups can connect directly with customers, suppliers and investors

---

[2] Mckinsey (2014). *Global Flows in a Digital Age*. Edited by James Manyika, Jacques Bughin, Susan Lund, Olivia Nottebohm, David Poulter, Sebastian Jauch, and Sree Ramaswamy. New York, NY: McKinsey Global Institute.

around the world. The free flow of data is a key driver of innovation by enabling the flow of new ideas, information and the sharing of knowledge.

Of the stages of the digital revolution, the emergence of the Internet was probably one of the biggest shifts.

The Age of the Internet

The Internet is considered to be one of the most relevant, powerful and influential inventions in human history. It has brought a revolution along with it. Nowadays we can hardly conceive life without the Internet, and over 3.4 billion people across the world use it. The digital communication flow between countries, businesses and citizens, as a component of the "knowledge economy," is recognized as a critical driver of economic growth and productivity. Internet protocol (IP) traffic continues to advance rapidly, with 2019 traffic projected to be 64 times its 2005 volume.[3] This cumulative growth impacts all facets of national economies, not just their budding technology sectors – in fact, an estimated 75% of the Internet's benefit is captured by businesses in traditional industries.[4]

Although the Internet was developed during the 1970s by the US Department of Defense, it did not reach its currently recognizable form until 1990. The Internet is a global network consisting of interconnected networks, in which millions of computers can communicate with each other via dedicated routers and servers. The Internet remained under government control until 1984. In 1989, Tim Berners-Lee invented the World Wide Web (WWW or Web for short) at the European Organization for Nuclear Research (CERN) in Switzerland. The Web is a global information space where users can create, read and share documents (identified by URLs (uniform (or universal) resource locators) and formatted with Hypertext Markup Language (HTML)), interlinked by hypertext links and accessed via the Internet utilizing the Hypertext Transfer Protocol (HTTP). We typically access the Web through Web browsers such as Google Chrome,

---

[3] Cisco Visual Networking Index: Global Mobile Data Traffic Forecast Update, 2015–2020, White Paper, http://www.cisco.com/c/en/us/solutions/collateral/service-provider/visual-networking-index-vni/mobile-white-paper-c11-520862.html.

[4] Pélissié du Rausas, M., Manyika, J., Hazan, E., Bughin, J., Chui, M., Said, R. (2011). *Internet Matters: The Net's Sweeping Impact on Growth, Jobs, and Prosperity*, McKinsey Global Institute, *Insights and Publications*. http://www.mckinsey.com/industries/high-tech/our-insights/internet-matters.

Mozilla Firefox or Internet Explorer. In the early 1990s, the Internet was globally deployed with the World Wide Web running on that infrastructure, in large part for commercial purposes.

In the early 1990s, businesses started creating home pages where they could place text and graphics to display information about their products and services, and other relevant business information. This first generation of the Web is called Web 1.0, also known as the informational or "read only" Web. Initially, Internet users could only read and share information over Web pages: websites were static and there was no interactive content. The creation of Web pages was done by software experts and was mostly proprietary. The next phase was Web 2.0, which provided a read/write networking platform, where users could communicate with each other. This evolved into the social media phase.

The next step in Internet and Web evolution is called Web 3.0, also known as the semantic Web. Contrary to Web 2.0, which uses the Internet to make connections between people, Web 3.0 uses the Internet to make connections with information. Thus, it is semantic, meaning data driven and personalized, as are My Yahoo, Google and so on. Web 3.0 not only searches for the user's keyword requests but also interprets the context of user requests, adjusting the results to meet the needs of the user.

In recent years, the Internet has moved from an essentially fixed network to a network accessed from mobile devices, using remote Wi-Fi connections as well as data connections using mobile communication networks. The boom in Internet usage via mobile devices stems from the paramount success of Apple's iPhone, followed by the emergence of a wave of smartphones. These devices have allowed mobile Internet services to become more user friendly.

The SMAC Revolution

SMAC is the acronym for social, mobile, analytics and cloud computing. SMAC's four emerging technologies combine to drive business innovation, growth and success. Together they develop a digital ecosystem that enables businesses to improve their business operations and better understand, interact and get closer to their customers. Furthermore, the massive adoption of mobile devices, Internet of Things sensors and heavy use of social media and website browsing creates a huge amount of structured and unstructured customer data, which allows the development of new business models. The creation of business value through the use of SMAC should focus on the synergies created by adopting the four technologies.

While the use of social media has completely changed how businesses connect, interact and engage with their customers, mobile devices have changed the ways in which people communicate, interact, buy and work. Both mobile and social media have certainly altered the ways in which purchasing decisions are made. Analytics (data analytics) helps businesses to understand customer buying behavior (how, when and where) and as a result develop new products and services to match that behavior. Finally, cloud computing services provide an efficient and agile way to access technology processing resources and data on demand, and help businesses to quickly adapt to changing markets by adjusting internal business processes and value propositions. However, the competitive advantage of SMAC implementations comes from the convergence of the four technologies.

A successful case of SMAC implementation is Netflix, the multinational entertainment company. SMAC has helped the company understand customer habits and preferences, and generate new products. For instance, when a Netflix member wants to stream a Netflix TV show from his/her mobile device, Netflix allows him/her to sign in via a Facebook account. After watching a show, Netflix members can use the multiple feedback tools that are offered. Users are encouraged to rate content with stars, write reviews and/or share what they have just watched with friends on Facebook or Twitter. Netflix uses the cloud to store all customer data and uses several analytics tools to understand customer behavior and to provide personalized recommendations and suggestions for each user, a concept known as one-to-one marketing (also 1:1 marketing or one-off marketing).

The New Consumer

Customers are rapidly embracing digital channels (e.g. email, Web, social media and mobile devices), and want to use them to acquire products and services and to interact with businesses. Nowadays, before contacting a sales representative, many customers routinely search online and collect information, check and conduct peer reviews, and compare prices and offers by using price comparison sites or manually from a multitude of information sources. In terms of customer service and support, telephone remains consumers' standard preference, but customers are now demanding self-service options as well as digital customer support through social

Table 1.2 New buyer types

Buyer type	Definition
Basic digital consumers	• Comfortable making online purchases. • Use of Web search, retail sites and brand sites. • Not highly mobile or social. • Buy in much the same way that most consumers did back in the "good old days."
Retail scouts	• Fast purchase decisions (averaging only three steps per purchase). • Prefer Web search and retail sites to brand sites. • Likely to use mobile and tablet devices. • The most receptive group to digital coupons.
Brand scouts	• Make quick decisions. • Great reliance on paid search but prefer specific brand sites to retail sites (and thus are more loyal as a rule). • Less likely to base their decisions on price. • Check features such as free shipping and money-back guarantees.
Digitally driven	• Highly mobile and social. • Value convenience and will go to great lengths to avoid going to a store. • More favorable to advertisements.
Calculated shoppers	• Long purchase decisions. • Analyze all the options carefully to get the best deal. • Likely to be "showroomers." • Use their mobile device to compare prices when they are close to a purchase. • Highly likely to use search. • Responsive to advertising that offers discounts and specials.
Eternal shoppers	• Smallest group. • Extremely long purchase decisions (up to 33 steps).

Source: Group M, 2013

media channels, online chat and email. By enabling and optimizing their customer digital channels, some businesses are creating new opportunities and value through connecting, interacting and engaging with their customers.

In 2013, GroupM,[5] the world's largest media investment group, analyzed a dataset of more than 168,000 purchases of consumer electronics. It found that there are six types of digital buyers. Each relies on some digital channels more than others, and takes a varying number of steps prior to making their purchases (see Table 1.2).

---

[5] GroupM next study illuminates the evolving role of Digital in the consumer journey, White paper, May 2013 http://www.wpp.com/wpp/press/2013/may/30/groupm-next-study-illuminates-evolving-role-of-digital-in-the-consumer-journey/.

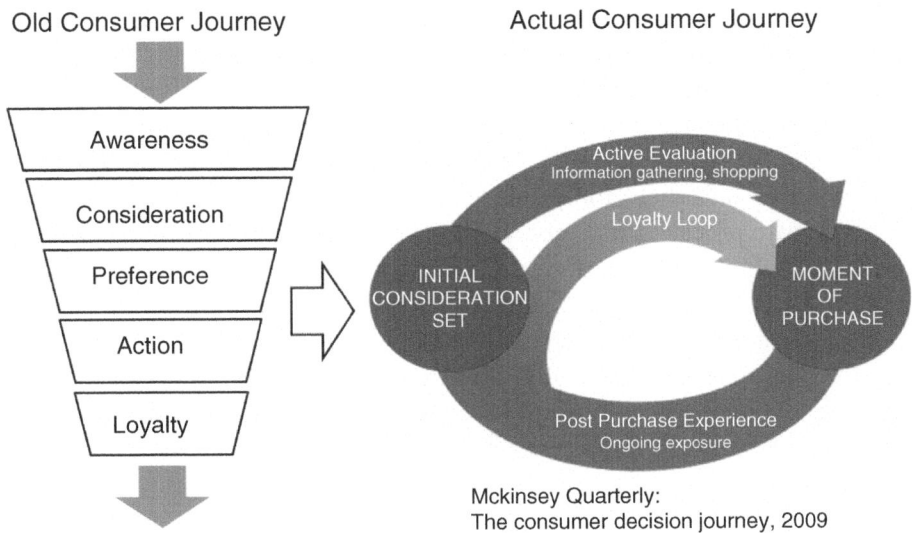

Fig. 1.1   The old and new customer decision journey

Consumer buying behavior has also changed, from the funnel approach (where customers followed a sequential buying process) to a more complex and dynamic method (see Fig. 1.1).

The incorporation of smartphones and the Internet in everyday life has driven the shift from passive to empowered customers, who have the ability to get what they want from anywhere, at any place and at any time. All this has not only created new customer behavior but has also affected consumers' daily purchase decisions. Today, customers can move through the shopping journey independently. Once linear, this shopping journey has evolved into a complex grid of touchpoints, interactions and communications with the customer at its heart.

This new approach allows businesses to creatively and effectively interact with their customers. Basing their response on Web, mobile and social media tools, businesses can use new digital marketing strategies to engage with consumers through more relevant and richer content. A good example is the "Share a Coke" campaign by Coca-Cola, where the name "Coca-Cola" was replaced in the bottle on one side by the phrase "Share a Coke with" followed by a person's name. Coca-Cola created interactive billboards, websites and traveling kiosks where people could get more uniquely named Coke products. At the same time, Coca-Cola encouraged users to share their stories and photos on social media. The campaign significantly increased sales and online engagement with the brand, this including 25 million additional Facebook followers.

Finally, the adoption of new digital channels allows consumers to make more informed consumption choices and increase their buying power. This is referred to as the prosumer movement. Consumers do not simply buy products, they also share and produce information about those products and help to create products and services. Prosumers can significantly impact the success or failure of those products, brands and businesses.

Web influencers – bloggers, microbloggers, YouTubers, social networking participants and so on, who spread messages – are affecting the decisions of many people all around the world. Many businesses leaders and marketers are not only identifying, following and respecting them, but they are also developing relationships that spread the word about their products, services and brands.

Business Digitization

To meet new high customer expectation, traditional businesses have started to accelerate their digitization. As previously mentioned, e-commerce has been one of the most salient aspects of the digital revolution. New online marketplaces such as eBay and Amazon have become household names, and rival the sales of even some of the largest traditional retail businesses.

In 2014, global e-commerce retail sales exceeded $1.3 trillion (around 5.9% of the total retail market, and nearly 2% of global GDP).[6] E-commerce growth has been driven by (i) a heavier use of online advertising, (ii) diffusion in social media, especially social networks, (iii) data collection process automation (which enables price comparison), (iv) smartphone adoption and (v) a larger number of online businesses with global or national coverage. China and the United States accounted for 55% of the global e-commerce retail market, primarily through leading online marketplaces such as Alibaba, eBay and Amazon.

In response to this growth, many retailers are embracing the omni-channel approach and enhancing the customer journey from purchasing to

---

[6] Retail Sales Worldwide Will Top $22 Trillion This Year, e-marketer 2014, http://www.emarketer.com/Article/Retail-Sales-Worldwide-Will-Top-22-Trillion-This-Year/1011765#sthash.aQyVR2rf.dpuf.

distribution to the "in-store experience." Furthermore, retailers that implement data analytics solutions to analyze customer data can increase retail operating margins by as much as 60%, higher than in any other industry.[7] E-commerce has become easy, quick, cool, efficient and convenient, and it has become the preferred method of shopping for many customers.

The current challenge of e-commerce platforms is how to handle inventory to keep up with customer service demands. Additionally, the growth of online sales has led to increased competition in delivery services.

In order to remain competitive, many businesses are investing in digital transformation initiatives. Their goal is to optimize business operations in order to be more efficient and sustainable, and at the same time be more customer-oriented, providing better experiences and engagement. The four titans of the Internet age, Google, Apple, Facebook and Amazon, which have been at the forefront of the digital revolution, are amazing examples of this change.

The Case of Amazon

In 1994, the 30-year-old Jeff Bezos founded Amazon in Seattle. The website was launched in July 1995 initially as an online bookstore, but Bezos's vision included the creation of "an everything store." Initially he opted to sell books because of their low cost, the enormous selection of available titles, universal demand and easy shipment.

The initial startup capital came primarily from his parents' savings. Bezos has said that his parents did not believe in the company or the concept, but they believed in their son.[8] In the coming years the company made a series of equity funding rounds.

Within two months of launch, Amazon's sales were up to $20,000 per week. However, the company has continued to plow its revenue back into growth. Amazon.com went public in 1997. Traditional bookstores responded with their own websites but none was as appealing, as agile or as successful as Amazon's. The company diversified its product catalogue first with CDs and videos, followed by electronic goods, toys and clothes. Sales leapt from half a million dollars in 1995 to $17 billion in 2011. Amazon pioneered many innovative practices, such as customer recommendation

---

[7] Getting big impact from big data, McKinsey Quarterly, January 2015, http://www.mckinsey.com/business-functions/business-technology/our-insights/getting-big-impact-from-big-data.

[8] Jeff Bezos Interview, Academy of Achievement http://www.achievement.org/autodoc/page/bez0int-4.

service and selling secondhand books. In order to maintain a consistent level of growth, Amazon has developed an impressive IT architecture and a wide range of skills, in the process becoming one of the leaders in cloud computing, with its AWS (Amazon Web Services) cloud computing service and in the use of big data technology. Amazon has continued to innovate in a remarkable number of fields such as drones, artificial intelligence, robotics and the aerospace industry.

Here are some of the most important milestones in Amazon's history:

- 1994: Jeff Bezos quits his job and launches Amazon out of his garage.

  – Within 30 days, it is doing $20,000 per week in sales.

- 1995: Amazon closes an $8 million round of funding with Kleiner Perkins.
- 1997: Amazon goes public with an IPO (initial public offering) price of $18 on May 15, 1997.
- 1999: Jeff Bezos is featured as *Time* magazine's "Person of the Year" for popularizing online shopping.
- 2005: Launch of the Amazon Prime premium membership service, which includes a variety of delivery benefits.
- 2006: Launch of AWS, a cloud computing platform.
- 2009: Bezos buys Zappos, an online shoe store, for $940 million in a stock and cash deal.
- 2011: Kindle Fire tablet is unveiled.
- 2012: Amazon acquires Kiva, a robotics company, for $775 million.
- 2013: Jeff Bezos acquires the *Washington Post*.
- 2015: Amazon celebrates its 20th birthday with market capitalization standing in excess of $245 billion.

The Case of Google

The story of Google started in 1995, when Larry Page, a 22-year-old graduate of the University of Michigan, and Sergey Brin, who was working on his doctorate in computer science, met at Stanford, California. Soon, they began collaborating on a Web search engine called BackRub, which operated on Stanford servers for more than a year before eventually taking up too much bandwidth.

In June 1999, the company issued its first press release to announce a $25 million equity funding round led by Sequoia Capital and Kleiner Perkins & Byers. In the press release, the company identified itself as a "start-up dedicated to providing the best search experience on the web," and also used the term "Googlers" in reference to Google employees. Michael Moritz, Sequoia Capital general partner, said that "Google should become the gold standard for search on the Internet." Here are the most important Google milestones:[9]

- 1995: Larry Page and Sergey Brin meet at Stanford.
- 1997: Google.com is registered as a domain on September 15.
- 1998: Google is officially established as a company on September 27.
- 1999: On June 7, 1999, Google issues its first press release to announce that it has raised $25 million in equity funding.
- 2000: In October, Google launches AdWords, its advertising network based on keyword targeting.
- 2001: Google Images is launched in July, initially offering users the ability to search through 250 million images.
- 2002: Google launches Google News with 4,000 news sources and Froogle, an ability to search for retail products that eventually became Google Shopping.
- 2004: Google's initial public offering takes place on August 19 and raises $1.67 billion on the NASDAQ stock exchange. Google launches the email service Gmail.
- 2005: Google launches Google Maps and Google Earth.
- 2006: On October 9, Google announces that it is to purchase YouTube for $1.65 billion
- 2007: In November, Google announces Android, the first open platform for smartphone mobile operating systems.
- 2008: In September, Google Chrome becomes available for download, and T-Mobile announces the first phone built with the Android OS (operating system).
- 2010: The Nexus One is launched in January, the first in Google's Nexus line of mobile devices.
- 2011: Larry Page takes over as chief executive officer (CEO) of Google in April, and announces the company's first Chromebook laptops in May. Google launches its own social network, Google+, in November.
- 2012: Google buys Motorola mobility for $12.5 billion.

---

[9] Google: our story in depth, https://www.google.com/about/company/history/.

- 2013: Google buys Israeli map app Waze for $1.15 billion.
- 2014: Google acquires Nest, a startup dedicated to create smart home devices such as thermostats, for $3.2 billion.
- 2015: Google creates Alphabet, a new umbrella company: subsidiaries are moved from Google to Alphabet.

The Case of Facebook

In February 4, 2004, online social networking platform Facebook was first launched as a Harvard social networking site. It was developed by 19-year-old Mark Zuckerberg with his Harvard College roommates and fellow students Eduardo Saverin, Andrew McCollum, Dustin Moskovitz and Chris Hughes. Initially called thefacebook.com, the site was an immediate success. Nowadays, it has become one of the biggest websites in the world, with over 1.71 billion monthly active users.

Mark Zuckerberg and Eduardo Saverin provided the initial investment to pay to launch the site and cover its operation costs. They also started publishing a few advertisements to help with these costs. In the summer of 2004, Facebook received $500,000 (10.2% of the company) from venture capitalist Peter Thiel, and he also joined Facebook's board. In May 2005, Thiel and Accel Partners paid $12.7 million for a 15% stake, helping to raise the valuation of Facebook to $87.5 million and 5.5 million active users. In April 2006, Facebook closed its Series B funding round of $27.5 million from a number of venture capitalists. The valuation reported for this round was $525 million.

In October 2007, Microsoft invested $240 million in Facebook for a 1.6% stake in the social network based on a $15 billion valuation. Microsoft purchased preferred stock, which gave the company some special rights, such as "liquidation preferences," which means that if Facebook is sold, Microsoft will be paid before common stockholders. The purchase also extended the companies' advertising partnership, by including Microsoft's right to sell advertisements for Facebook internationally. In 2008, Hong Kong billionaire Li Ka-shing purchased a 0.8% stake in Facebook for $120 million.

Facebook held its IPO on May 18, 2012, one of the biggest IPOs in Internet history: it reached an original peak market capitalization of $104 billion. Since 2005, Facebook has spent $22 billion acquiring more than 50 companies, including digital companies such as Instagram, WhatsApp and Oculus VR. On July 13, 2015, Facebook surpassed Google as the fastest company in the Standard & Poor's (S&P) 500 Index to go from IPO to a $250 billion market cap.

Digital Capabilities

The digital age is quickly forcing companies to transform their business operations and strategy, and one of the key issues is rethinking and developing the new (digital) capabilities to enable a successful digital transformation. With these new capabilities, businesses can adjust quickly to change by becoming more agile, connected and sustainable. Thus, digital capabilities is understood as an umbrella term that defines the set of capabilities required in order to compete in the digital world, including digital leadership, technology skills (SMAC), digital governance, innovation, collaboration, change management and some technological capabilities, such as unified technology platform, data analytics, and business and IT integration.

Digital Economy

The extent and speed of the digital revolution's effect on society will continue to change the structure of the economy as we know it and will force businesses to transition from the old economy to a new one, known as the digital economy (sometimes called the Internet economy, Web economy or network economy). All these terms refer to a new global economic system that is based on digital technologies, including the Internet, social networks and online marketing.

Table 1.3 shows a snapshot of the evolution of the largest businesses per market capitalization over the last ten years. In 2006, the energy sector was king, with Exxon and General Electric at the top of the list. Five years later, in 2001, when oil prices soared to the $100/bbl (per barrel), three of the five

Table 1.3 Evolution of largest businesses per market capitalization over the last ten years

Ranking	2006	2011	2016
1	Exxon – $446B	Exxon – $406B	Apple – $582B
2	General Electric – $383B	Apple – $376B	Alphabet – $556B
3	Total – $327B	PetroChina – $277B	Microsoft – $452B
4	Microsoft – $293B	Shell – $237B	Amazon – $364B
5	Citi – $273B	KBC – $228B	Facebook – $359B

largest businesses by market capitalization were in the oil business: Exxon, PetroChina and Royal Dutch Shell. In 2016, with the oil price at $40/bbl, no energy businesses crack the top five. Instead, the list has been completely replaced by tech businesses, including Apple, Alphabet, Amazon, Facebook and Microsoft, which are leading the so-called new digital capitalism. This reinforces the growing importance of the digital economy and helps to identify some future trends. Apple and Google/Alphabet not only represent the rise of the digital economy, but also drive business and digital innovation. In 1998, Google was officially founded and Apple was valued at $4.1 billion after flirting with bankruptcy. The technology sector is dominated by US-domiciled businesses.

The digital economy goes beyond the digitization of traditional business operations and models. It is transforming every aspect of modern life: entertainment, health, education, work and citizen participation in government decision-making and policymaking. The three main components that make up the digital economy are:[10]

- Technology infrastructure (hardware, software, telecoms, networks, etc.).
1. E-business (how business is conducted, any business process that takes place over computer-mediated networks).
2. E-commerce (online trading of goods and services).

The positive effects of the digital economy can be seen on countless fronts, from increased economic activity to improved quality of life throughout society. The flagship of the digital revolution has been the invention of the Internet, which has interconnected the world and promoted globalization.

Data flows accounted for US$2.8 trillion of global GDP in 2014, with cross-border data flows generating more economic value than traditional flows.[11] Cross-border flows (data and voice, in particular) reduce costs related to both trade and transactions. This includes customer engagement (finding and fulfilling orders) as well as other operational costs associated with doing business. One recent report by the US International Trade Commission (ITC) estimates that the Internet reduces trade costs by an average of 26%.[12] Additionally, small

---

[10] Mesenbourg, T.L. (2001). *Measuring of the Digital Economy. The Netcentric Economy Symposium.* University of Maryland.
[11] McKinsey (2016). *Digital Globalization: The New Era of Global Flows, Mckinsey Global Institute Report*, http://www.mckinsey.com/business-functions/digital-mckinsey/our-insights/digital-globalization-the-new-era-of-global-flows.

and medium-sized enterprises that use the Internet to trade on global platforms have a survival rate of 54%, which is 30% higher than that of offline businesses.

By way of an example that quantifies the significance of the digital revolution for the economy, a recent report by the Internet Association shows that in 2014 the Internet sector accounted for 6% of GDP ($966.2 billion) – double the figure in 2007.[13] The role now played by the Internet and other digital technologies in economic activity has not only affected the "pure" sectors born in the digital revolution (e.g. Google and Facebook) but all other sectors too.

The World Economic Forum developed the Networked Readiness Index (NRI), also called the Technology Readiness Index, which measures on a scale from one (worst) to seven (best) how well an economy is exploiting the opportunities offered by IT. Currently, the NRI measures the performance of 139 countries.

NRI gathers its data from international organizations such as the World Bank, the International Telecommunication Union, the United Nations Educational, Scientific and Cultural Organization (UNESCO) and other United Nations agencies. Further indicators come from the Executive Opinion Survey (World Economic Forum), which was completed by over 14,000 business executives in more than 140 countries. NRI evaluates if a country has the drivers to exploit its digital technology potential, and the current impact of digital technology on the economy and society.

To get an accurate picture of all the drivers and the full effects, the study breaks down the information into different subsections (see Fig. 1.2).

One of the key findings of the 2016 NRI index is that the digital revolution is changing the nature of innovation, which is relying more and more on digital technologies and new Web business models. The findings also show that most of the development of digital capacities is focused on wealthy countries. Seven countries stand out in terms of the economic impact of their corporate digitization: Finland, Switzerland, Sweden, Israel, Singapore, the Netherlands and the United States. It is noticeable that all seven are characterized by very high levels of business IT adoption.

A resilient digital economy calls for new types of behavior, leadership and governance. In that sense, the NRI helps to identify which policies are

---

[12] US ITC (2014). Digital Trade in the U.S. and Global Economies, Part 2, United States International Trade Commission, https://www.usitc.gov/publications/332/pub4485.pdf.

[13] Internet Association. (2015). Measuring the U.S. internet sector, Business report http://internetasso ciation.org/wp-content/uploads/2015/12/Internet-Association-Measuring-the-US-Internet-Sector-12-10-15.pdf.

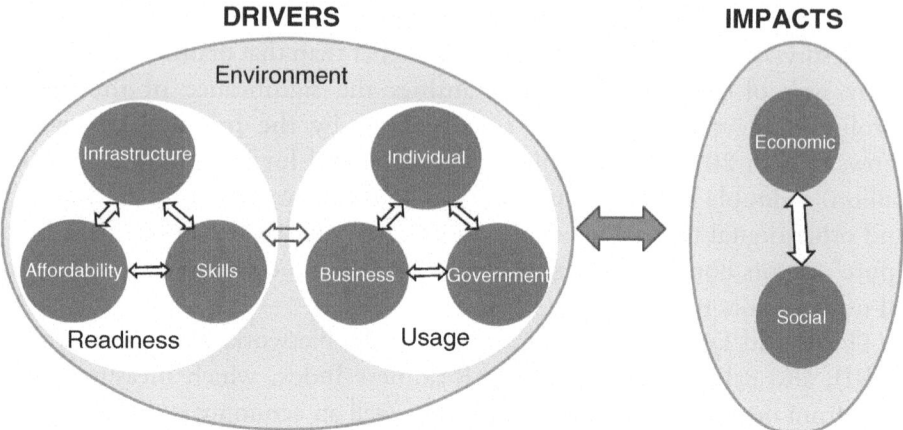

Fig. 1.2   The networked readiness framework

Source: World Economic Forum. Global Information Technology Report 2015, World Economic Forum, http://reports.weforum.org/global-information-technol ogy-report-2015/

working and which are not, which countries are leading the way and which need to do more.

The impact of digital technologies is influenced by factors such as broadband network infrastructure coverage, the dissemination and use of digital technologies by individuals and businesses, and their incorporation into operational and organizational processes. Various studies show that private consumption represents the largest part of the Internet's contribution to GDP and it is greater in the emerging economies.

Web Business Models

Internet and Web technologies have created the possibility to create new business models. Typically, there are three main types of Web business models: business-to-consumer (B2C), business-to-business (B2B) and consumer-to-consumer (C2C). Websites following B2C and B2B business models typically sell goods and services and/or provide information to help users research and make purchase decisions. C2C models allow customers to interact with each other, and they involve C2C information or goods and services exchange.

As Michael Rappa says, "in the most basic sense, a business model is the method of doing business by which a company can sustain itself – that is, generate revenue."[14] Based on the revenue model perspective, he has defined a taxonomy of the main Web business models, identifying nine different types.

Since this is a book dealing with the economic effects of a digital world, Rappa's taxonomy is particularly useful in analyzing business under the perspective of economic value, keeping in mind that the generation of revenue is the first step to make a company feasible and profitable from an economic point of view.

The most commonly used Web business models are described below with some examples. In most of these cases, businesses combine different revenue models as part of their digital business strategy. For instance, it is quite common for content-driven businesses to combine a community model with an advertising model.

Merchant and Brokerage Models

The merchant model is a very popular Web business model amongst online wholesalers and retailers. It consists in selling goods or services over the Internet using a list of prices or via an auction. Merchant models can be categorized as:

1. E-tailer (also called online merchant or virtual merchant): wholesale and retail businesses that operate solely over the internet. Examples of e-tailers include Amazon.com or Ocado (UK pure online supermarket).
2. Bit vendor: a merchant that exclusively sells digital goods or services over the internet. One example is the Apple iTunes music store.
3. Click and mortar: businesses that include both online and offline operations, they typically have an online shop and a physical store. Some examples include Zara, Macys and Walmart.
4. Catalog merchant: businesses where users selected products from a Web-based catalog and then order them using Web, email or telephone. Examples include Argos (UK based, general-goods) or Land's End (US based, clothing).

A broker brings together buyers and sellers and usually charges a fee or commission (e.g. percentage of the transaction price) for each transaction. Examples of the brokerage model include eBay, Priceline, Orbitz and

---

[14] Michael Rappa, Business Models on the Web, http://digitalenterprise.org/models/models.html.

Amazon. These are the major types of brokers (source: Board of Innovation):[15]

1. Marketplace: provides a broad or dedicated platform on which sellers can list their offers, buyers can look for interesting offers and both can finalize transactions. Example: Pro Merchant Subscription on Amazon.
2. Auction broker: specific type of marketplace where auctions are organized for sellers (individuals or merchants). Usually charges a listing fee and/or commission per transaction. Example: eBay.
3. Payment broker: provides a payment system for buyers and sellers to complete a transaction. Example: PayPal.
4. Search catalog: offers buyers a search engine to search on availability and price of specific products or services. Examples: Kayak, Trivago.
5. Crowdbuying broker: leverages the buying power of a group of consumers to get a good deal.
6. Lending broker: brings together borrowers and lenders, and facilitates transactions. Known as peer-to-peer lending or social lending. Example: Zopa.

Community Model

This model is becoming extremely widespread. It is associated with community websites, and gathers a group of users around a common interest. They interact with each other by sharing information and making contributions to their online communities. Web communities can be public or private and there are different types, such as social network services, online forums, a single blog or group of blogs, video- and photo-sharing platforms. Usually, this Web business model is combined with other models, such as advertising, subscription or freemium. Alternatively, some community models ask for donations (e.g. Wikipedia).

The community model can be B2C or B2B, and it is implemented in most C2C Web business models. The major players include social networking platforms, Facebook, Google+, Renren (Chinese social network), Twitter and LinkedIn, editorial content sites such as Mashable and Buzzfeed, and user-generated content sites such as eHow, Quora, YouTube and Wikipedia. Other community model types include discussion lists (moderated and

---

[15] The broker variants and examples, the Board of Innovation http://www.boardofinnovation.com/business-revenue-model-examples/the-broker/.

unmoderated lists) and reader-participation blogs. The key characteristic of all these models is a focus on individuals talking to each other and sharing information and experiences, rather than unidirectional communication from businesses to users/consumers.

Infomediary Model

This model makes money by selling information products. The term is a composite of "information" and "intermediary." Infomediary agents independently aggregate data about producers, their products and services, and their current and potential customers; then they analyze it to provide insights that help buyers and sellers understand a given market. The four main types of infomediary model are: advertising networks (e.g. Sharethis, Doubleclick), audience measurement (e.g. Alexa, Nielsen and ComScore), incentive marketing (e.g. coolsavings) and metamediary (e.g. ivillage.ca, related to women's issues such as pregnancy, health and parenting, or Edmunds, an automobile information site).

Affiliate Model

The affiliate model allows online businesses to offer third party products and services to their users in return of a commission. In the majority of the cases, they may never actually take ownership of the product (or even handle it). An example is Amazon's affiliate program, Amazon Associates, which helps individual websites link to specific products offered by Amazon and earn up to 15% commission. Usually this model works very well for websites with a large volume of traffic.

Advertising Model

This model is an amplification of the traditional advertising model. It employs the Internet to deliver paid advertising messages to consumers by using many types of display advertising (e.g. text advertisements, video, images, search placement and Web banners). There are four basic pricing models: cost per impression, revenue share, cost per click, and cost per acquisition deals.

Google is the most famous and successful example of this model, which is more successful for highly specialized websites or where there is a large volume of viewer traffic. The model is mostly used by portals (e.g. Yahoo), query-based paid placement (e.g. Google), classifieds (e.g. Monster.com), user registration (e.g. the *New York Times* newspaper), content-targeted advertising (Google) and contextual advertising (About.com).

Manufacturer's Direct Model

This model, also called the factory model, entails a manufacturer selling its products directly to the consumer. The model's efficacy relies on the ability of the manufacturer to sell directly to the customer while removing retail intermediaries, thus shortening the distribution channel. Two famous examples are Dell (computers) and Cisco (electronic components). In a further development of the model, Dell gives consumers the option to customize products according to their needs.

Subscription Model

In this model, the customer must pay a daily, weekly or monthly subscription fee to have access to information or a digital service. This has gained popularity primarily because of its use by newspapers and magazine sites. Nowadays, it is used by many businesses and websites, such as Netflix and Spotify. The advantage of this model is the flexibility offered to the customer, because it gives the ability to decide when to pay and to cancel a subscription at any time. For businesses the advantage is a constant and ongoing revenue stream. Many news sites and content aggregators use this model.

Utility Model

In this model the customer pays based on specific usage rates via a "pay as you go" approach. It charges according to how much is used rather than a fixed weekly/monthly fee. This model is quite common in software as a service (SaaS) businesses. An example of an SaaS business is Salesforce.com, where users pay a fee to access a customer relationship management Web-based software. Another example is AWS, through which Amazon offers a variety of cloud services, such as storage, computing and networking, databases, deployment and management, and application services. For each cloud service, the customers pays for exactly the amount of resources that are needed and used.

In many cases, utility and subscription model are combined. Some experts say that the utility model relates to what you offer and the subscription model relates to how you offer it.

Other Models: Freemium

Freemium is a Web business model that consists of a combination of "free" and "premium." It has become the dominant business model for many Web businesses, smartphone app developers and the video gaming industry.

The main goal of freemium is to attract a huge number of users who will use the product/service for nothing and later convince some of them to pay for additional features (e.g. upgrades, advanced features and/or virtual goods). This model is also called "land and expand": you try to land with a freemium offer and expand with paid offers. The key advantage of this model is that it allows customers to explore and engage with your product. Some freemium examples include Skype, LinkedIn, Dropbox, Hulu and dating sites such as Match. As the CEO of Dropbox said, "The fact was that Dropbox was offering a product that people didn't know they needed until they tried."

Table 1.4 presents a summary of the main Web business models with some examples.

Table 1.4 Summary of main Web business models

Business model	Brief description	Examples
Brokerage	Brings sellers and buyers together	Alibaba, eBay
Advertising	Delivers messages with content	Google, Yahoo
Infomediary	Resells useful data	Nielsen
Merchant	Sells goods and services	Amazon
Manufacturer	Approaches buyers directly	Dell
Affiliate	Offers incentives to affiliated partner sites	Amazon
Community	Connects individuals and groups/communities	Facebook
Subscription	Offers services and content for a set fee	Salesforce, Netflix
Utility	Offers services or content on a "pay as you go" basis	Dropbox, AWS
Freemium	Offers service or content for free and offer premium priced value added services	LinkedIn, Skype, Dropbox

Sharing Economy

The Internet is always evolving, and one of the emergent areas is the digital sharing economy, also known as collaborative consumption or the peer economy. These terms are used to describe economic and social activity that involves online transactions related to sharing and reusing resources.

Sharing economy businesses are organized around Web platforms that bring together individuals who have underused physical and digital resources with people who would like to rent or freely share those resources. For example, Airbnb allows individuals to rent out a room or an entire apartment; BlaBlaCar, a ride-sharing app, allows users to advertise empty seats on their journeys between cities.

The sharing economy relies on social media and in many ways is a logical expansion of social media platforms such as Facebook, Instagram and Trip Advisor. Before social media, users didn't tend to share on the Web. Developments in social media have also brought more transparency and trust, which are key factors in using sharing economy services. Sharing economy businesses (e.g. Uber, Airbnb) are considered to be business platforms because they don't own the resources used; they only act as intermediaries between consumers. However, these new types of models have raised difficult legal, tax, labor and social questions. As the sharing economy matures, governments will need to address the risks and challenges that this inevitably brings.

Summary

1. The use of digital technology is increasing day by day. The integration of digital technology into everyday life has a range of consequences for individuals, families, communities, governments and businesses.
2. This digital revolution, known as the Third Industrial Revolution, is the change from analogue, mechanical and electronic technology to digital technology.
3. Customers are rapidly adopting new channels – including Web, social media and mobile.

4. To meet the high expectations of their consumers, many businesses have started to accelerate the digitization of their business processes and are adopting e-commerce as a key component of their sales strategy.
5. The digital economy refers to an economy that is based on digital technologies, although we increasingly perceive this as conducting business through markets based on the Internet and the Web.
6. The Internet and the Web have allowed the development and/or expansion of new business models.
7. In the most basic sense, a business model is the method of doing business by which a company can sustain itself – that is, generate revenue. Based on the revenue model perspective, we can define a taxonomy of the main Web business models, identifying ten different types.

It should come as no surprise that the continuing development of the Internet consistently results in significant shifts as to how businesses operate, how consumers react and how products are bought and sold. Naturally, the very fundamental structures of business models continue to evolve in line with this, becoming far more flexible and innovative than ever before. An example of this is the emergence of the digital sharing economy.

2

Economic Value and Digital Business

Introduction

In the previous chapter we dealt with business, the digital world, digital models and digital business models in order to clarify these concepts and set up an analytical framework to better understand digital business.

In this chapter we are going to discuss whether and how digital business creates economic value (EV). Since we already know about digital business, let's begin by explaining what EV is.

What Is EV?

Sometimes, in order to understand what something is, it is useful to clarify what it is not. Let's use this approach to get a better understanding of the concept of EV.

What EV Is Not

EV is not just a qualitative value, as, for example, sentimental value is. A house may be of great sentimental value but have very little EV; or the other way round.

EV is not just an accounting value. A company may have a substantial accounting value but a less spectacular EV. Why? Because the accounting

© The Author(s) 2017   27
F.J. López Lubián, J. Esteves, *Value in a Digital World*,
DOI 10.1007/978-3-319-51750-6_2

value deals with historical information, presented in an accurate, systematic and consistent way, and EV covers the expected future and associated risks.

In fact, to go from accounting value to EV we have to consider three additional components:

1. Generation of real money (cash flows).
2. Expected future of the business.
3. Associated risks.

Furthermore, all measures of EV must include an appropriate conceptual and practical response to these three elements. In other words, in order to know whether a given management decision can create (or destroy) EV, we have to have a clear and reasonable answer as to how this decision will generate real money in a sustainable and differentiated way, and how we are going to deal with the risks that arise in an uncertain future.

At the end of the day, when dealing with EV we try to find a reasonable answer to the following question: what is the value of this? In other words, how much would you pay for this, considering its EV?

Measuring EV

There are two ways to measure EV.

First, we have the extrinsic EV, which is derived from what the market dictates.

Some people believe that the market provides the only possible and most realistic answer. If you adopt this approach, you believe that the market is the best mechanism to establish the EV of everything. In other words, you believe the market will provide supply and demand to determine a price, which will naturally include all adjustments, including the accounting value and the three additional elements required to set up a reasonable EV, or a price.

Are there any problems with using the extrinsic EV? There are, if we consider that this extrinsic EV (the price) is not the only and most realistic way in which to determine a reasonable EV. Extrinsic EV is certainly a reference to be considered, but it is not always the best way to arrive at a reasonable EV. In fact, a financial bubble occurs when the market is paying prices based on extrinsic EVs that are clearly unreasonable and unsustainable.

That's why we have to complement an extrinsic EV with an intrinsic EV. Using the intrinsic EV we try to capture the EV of something based on its accounting value and future business plans. In other words, we do not take for granted that the market price will naturally reflect the transition from accounting value to reasonable EV.

Using the intrinsic EV we estimate a reasonable EV by analyzing the expected future, sustainable and differential cash flows that the assets will generate, and by calculating the present value of those cash flows, using a discount rate which includes the value of money in terms of time, derived from opportunity costs, inflation and risks.

An example will help to clarify these important concepts.

An Example of Measuring EV

Let's assume that we want to estimate the EV of a digital company, CV1.

The company was founded in 2012 and operates in logistics.

As mentioned above, this company may have quite a different sentimental value, psychological value and ethical value, as well as other types of qualitative values. When focusing our analysis on quantitative value and EV, the right question to ask is:

What is a reasonable EV for CV1? How much should we pay for it?

Let's start with CV1's accounting value. Table 2.1 summarizes the company balance sheet at the end of 2015.

According to this information, the accounting value of CV1 is $250 million, with an accounting value for the equity of $225 million because the company has $25 million of debt.

Can we consider that this accounting value of $250 million is a reasonable EV? Most probably not, since EV is different from accounting value.

Let's assume that the company is a public company, listed on a capital market. At the end of 2015 the share price was $3. Knowing that the company has 500,000 shares, we can estimate that the extrinsic EV of the equity will be $1,500 million. Assuming also that the accounting and EV of

Table 2.1 Balance sheet of CV1

Net current assets	50	Debt	25
Net fixed assets	200	Equity	225
Total net assets	250	Debt + equity	250

Figures in millions US $

the debt are similar, then we can estimate that the extrinsic EV is $1,525 million (= 1,500 + 25).

Therefore, with a company accounting value of $250 million the market is providing an estimated EV of $1,525 million.

How can we know if this extrinsic EV will be sustainable? How can we determine whether this major difference between accounting value and EV is reasonable?

As noted above, we can estimate the intrinsic EV of CV1 by basing our figures on the business plan or on the company's strategy. Let's assume that after a careful analysis of the expected and reasonable future of the company, we believe that Table 2.2 is a reasonable summary of the differential and sustainable expected cash flows that CV1 will generate in the coming five years, including a terminal value (TV).

According to this information, the intrinsic EV of CV1 will be $865 million, since the expected TV at the end of Year 5 will be $700 million and a reasonable associated discount rate (weighted average cost of capital, WACC) is 8%.

Table 2.3 summarizes the different values of CV1's expected evolution of free cash flow (FCF).

Table 2.2 Expected evolution of FCF

Years		1	2	3	4	5
FCF		50	80	100	125	150
TV						700
Total FCF		50	80	100	125	850
WACC	8%					
EV	865					

Figures in millions US $

Table 2.3 Summary of values for CV1

Accounting value of CV1	250
Accounting value of the equity	225
Extrinsic economic value of CV1	1525
Extrinsic economic value of the equity	1500
Intrinsic economic value of CV1	865
Intrinsic economic value of the equity	840
Accounting price of a share	0.45 $/share
Price of the share	3.00 $/share
Intrinsic price of the share	1.68 $/share

Figures in millions of US $

EV in Practice: The Useful Questions

To create EV in digital business, and in any business for that matter, we have to generate enough differential and sustainable cash flows so that even when discounted at the minimum expected economic profitability desired by our providers of financial resources (debt and equity), the present value would still be positive and better than the alternatives.

Note that EV is a matter of cash flows and of rate of discount.

But what cash flows? And what rate of discount?

What Cash Flows?

The cash flows to be considered in the EV have to have the following characteristics:

(a) They must be real money, real cash flows; that is, involving a real movement of cash. In other words, we should ignore simple accounting entries that do not involve an actual payment of cash in or out.

(b) They must be forecasted cash flows; that is, referring to the future.

(c) They must be differential cash flows; that is, they must arise as a result of decisions made under analysis. In other words, if the cash flow in question will be generated regardless of the outcome of the decision you are considering, it makes no difference to the variation in value resulting from the decision. It is not "differential," and therefore should not be taken into account in the measurement of the creation of EV.

(d) They must be after-tax cash flows, since we are primarily interested in the creation of wealth for the company and not for the tax man.

(e) They must be sustainable cash flows; that is, they must last for a long period.

In practical terms, the difficulty can lie in determining whether a particular cash flow should be included in the analysis of EV creation for a given management decision. An example should clarify this point.

Let us suppose that, as a member of the investment committee of your company, you are involved in a meeting to decide whether or not to approve an investment in a new factory. One of the key factors in the decision is to ascertain whether the new factory will create EV. To do this, it will be necessary to include all the right cash flows and avoid any unnecessary ones.

During the meeting various members of the committee raise the following issues:

1. Although the land on which the factory is going to be built belongs to the company and the company has no other use for it, the fact that it is a prime location in an area undergoing industrial expansion means that its market value is considerable. Specifically, whereas the book value of the land is $50 million, it could currently be sold for $600 million. This difference of $550 million does not appear in the analysis of the project being considered, but it clearly represents a potential loss of income or opportunity cost for the company if the project is approved. As a result, according to the opinion of one of the members of the Board of Directors, this amount should be considered as a negative cash flow.
2. In addition to the fact that the land is valued at $600 million, improvements were recently made at a cost of $50 million, allowing better plant access to the location. As it would not be possible to consider the current investment if the improvement work had not been undertaken, this cost should also be included among the project's costs, in the opinion of another member of the board.
3. The figures on the table include a charge for depreciation calculated by taking advantage of the option to apply accelerated depreciation to this project. "Why is this being done?" asks a third member of the board. "By increasing depreciation we are reducing earnings; thus we are reducing the profitability of the project."
4. The same member points out: "On the other hand, the figures do not include a share of head office expenses. How could this oversight have occurred?"
5. Finally, in order to use this land to build the factory it will be necessary to demolish a number of existing buildings. The cost of demolition is included in the plans, but there is no mention of the loss caused. As these buildings have a book value of $10 million this sum should be included, according to another member of the board.

Clearly the list could be endless. The question is to decide whether these facts are relevant or not when measuring the EV produced by building the factory. Do they meet the requirements to be considered as cash flows for the project? Let's look at each of them in turn:

1. Market value versus book value: opportunity cost

Inappropriate use of the concept of opportunity cost is a frequent cause of decisions that destroy value. Opportunity cost must always be defined in the context of the real alternatives available. Postulating unreal or incomplete alternatives can lead to confusion, as at the end of the day everything can be considered to be an opportunity cost for something else. In the case we are considering, this market value is not a cash flow for the project, as in order to convert a market value into cash the land needs to be sold, in which case we don't have a factory. Selling the land is in fact a different investment project, which may compete with that we are considering, insofar as it would be an alternative use for one of the assets the company owns. The aim would therefore be to look at the value created by each of the mutually exclusive projects and choose the best one.

2. Sunk costs

This is another issue that can often lead to mistakes. Costs that have already been incurred and are irreversible cannot be a differentiating factor in analyzing the value created by a decision which has not yet been made. Why not? For the simple reason that the outlay took place before the decision was made. In this case, the cost of the improvement work is a sunk cost as the work has been paid for and the cost cannot be recovered, regardless of whether the factory is actually built. Thus, the decision should be made regardless of whether or not this money was well spent, which should have been analyzed at the time.

The fact that a sunk cost is not a differentiating factor in measuring the value created by a current decision does not mean it is totally irrelevant, nor that we should forget about it. The reasons for making the outlay need to be analyzed to see if the right decision was made, but this is independent from the current decision we face.

Is a cost already incurred always independent from the future generation of cash flows arising out of an investment? The answer to this question will be examined in the next section.

3. Depreciation expenses

As the reader is no doubt aware, the accounting concept of depreciation tries to reflect the physical decline in the value of an asset over time; that is, the loss of value as a result of its use. When a depreciation expense is recorded it is never treated as a cash flow, as it is an expense which does not directly involve either a present or a future payment. Does that mean that a difference in depreciation has no effect on future cash flows?

No, it does have an effect, insofar as there can be repercussions on corporate taxes paid. As depreciation expenses are tax deductible, if the company has positive taxable earnings in the years in which value creation is being analyzed, the amount of annual depreciation will affect the amount of tax paid. Although clearly over the whole period the same amount is paid in tax, it is also the case that accelerated depreciation delays payment of these taxes, thereby favoring value creation.

Table 2.4 shows an example applicable to the case in question. Assuming the investment is €300 million and the discount rate applicable is 10%, if an accelerated depreciation method is used – specifically in this case the sum of the years' digits method – instead of straight-line depreciation, additional value of around $12 million is created by deferring the tax liability. Obviously, for this to be so the company must have taxable earnings.

Table 2.4 Does depreciation create value?

Case A: Straight-line depreciation

	1	2	3	4	5	6	7	8	9	10
Earnings Before Interests Taxes and Depreciation and Amortization (EBITDA)	100	110	120	130	140	150	160	170	180	190
Depreciation	-30	-30	-30	-30	-30	-30	-30	-30	-30	-30
EBIT	70	80	90	100	110	120	130	140	150	160
Taxes (50%)	-35	-40	-45	-50	-55	-60	-65	-70	-75	-80
EBIaT	35	40	45	50	55	60	65	70	75	80
Operating FCF	65	70	75	80	85	90	95	100	105	110
Net Present Value (NPV) (10%)	513,85									
Average ROI	19.1%									

Case B: Accelerated depreciation

	1	2	3	4	5	6	7	8	9	10
EBITDA	100	110	120	130	140	150	160	170	180	190
Depreciation	55	-49	-44	-38	-33	-27	-22	-16	-11	-5
Earnings Before Interests and Taxes (EBIT)	45	61	76	92	107	123	138	154	169	185
Taxes (50%)	-23	-31	-38	-46	-54	-62	-69	-77	-84	93
EBIaT	22	30	38	46	53	61	69	77	85	92
Operating FCF	77	79	82	84	86	88	91	93	96	97
NPV (10%)	525,54									
Average ROI	19.1%									

Figures in millions of Euros

It is interesting to observe that if we applied an accounting value criterion to evaluate this decision, for example the average return on investment (ROI), the apparent value creation in each of the alternatives is the same, given that the average ROI is 19.2%. It can be seen that, once again, the right tools need to be used in order to obtain the right measurements.

We can now return to the question raised in the previous section. Insofar as a sunk cost may be capitalized and subsequently depreciated, it is the same case as the cost of depreciation. Hence, this sunk cost assigned to the future project can produce a differential cash flow over the next few years through a tax saving. What, then, are the conditions under which a sunk cost, although already paid and non-recoverable, can generate a different cash flow in a project? Basically, the following conditions have to be met:

1. It produces a cash flow; that is, it can be capitalized and offset against future earnings by depreciating it.
2. It is differential; that is, this capitalization and future depreciation can only take place if the project is carried out.

4. Allocated expenses

In order for an expense to be relevant to the measurement of the EV generated by a decision, the important thing is not that it can be allocated according to a particular accounting principle, but that it is differential: that it is incurred only if the decision is made. Therefore, if head office overheads will be incurred regardless of whether the factory is built or not, they are clearly not differential, although in accounting terms part of these overheads may be allocated to the new factory. On the other hand, if opening the new factory will bring with it an increase in turnover, making it necessary to hire more staff at head office, for instance, this expense would be differential, net of taxes. Moreover, if a reduction in the costs incurred by central office could be forecast in the case where the factory is not built, this reduction would be differential, net of taxes.

5. Sale of assets

The sale of an asset may result in a book loss or profit, as assets are not always sold for the book value they are allocated in the accounts. This book loss or profit is not a cash flow, although its tax repercussions do represent a cash flow if there is a positive tax liability to which a profit must be added or against which a loss can be offset.

Let's consider an example. An asset is sold for $5 million, whereas its book value is $10 million, resulting in a book loss of $5 million. This loss is not a cash flow, but it reduces the taxable earnings by $5 million,[1] thus resulting in a reduction in the company's tax payment of $1.75 million, given a tax rate of 35%. In this case the differential cash flow would be the collection of $5 million from the sale of the asset and a saving of $1.75 million in tax.

All disposals of assets should be handled in this way, whether they are fixed or current assets.

To summarize, in the case of any doubt as to whether any given economic fact should be included in the analysis of value creation for a given decision, we need to ask if this fact is:

1. Cash flow: it involves a real payment in or out.
2. Differential: it only takes place if the decision is made.
3. After taxes: it refers to the situation after the effect of tax has been taken into account.
4. Sustainable: it comes from a competitive advantage that will allow the company to keep generating these differential cash flows in the future.

Only if you have an affirmative answer to all these questions should the factor in question be included as a differential and sustainable cash flow, which will generate EV. The difficulty, therefore, tends not to be conceptual so much as practical: it is easy to miss cash flows that are differential.

To avoid this happening, it is worth pointing out a series of rules of thumb that are applicable to the economic analysis of any decision:

RULE I

Do not forget the initial outlay and any successive outlays that are needed to meet working capital requirements as a result of incremental investment in the working capital.

In fact, many investments in fixed assets result in an increase in the volume of business, thereby causing greater current asset requirements – in terms of customer receivables, inventory, cash in hand – and produce more

---

[1] Providing the company had enough taxable earnings.

finance from short-term liabilities – suppliers, creditors, deferred taxes and so on. The net result of these finance requirements and sources is a differential cash flow that needs to be considered in the decision-making process.

RULE II

Do not overlook the possible final liquidation of the working capital, including the eventual recovery of part of the initial investment. Any economic analysis has a time limit, even when the decision has no specific deadline: it would be a nuisance to continually have to draw up cash flow forecasts. There is therefore always a final year in the analysis, in which the possible liquidation of differential businesses has to be considered or their TV has to be estimated.

RULE III

Ignore sunk costs, those costs already paid and which cannot be recouped, unless they have a differential effect on tax liability. The past does not create EV, unless it teaches us how to make better decisions.

RULE IV

Do not confuse past cash flows with future cash flows. In other words, do not limit your forecasts to a slavish repetition of the past. It is usually the case that we are preparing a forecast precisely because we want the future to be better or we expect it to be different.

RULE V

Be systematic about analyzing cash flows. Practice shows that it is fairly easy to leave out elements that may be relevant.

Among other reasons, that's why to analyze EV creation most people use a very specific cash flow, defined in a very concrete way: the FCF. The FCF is the cash that comes from the assets, regardless of how they are financed. It reflects the capacity of the assets to generate liquidity per se, apart from how they are financed.

Table 2.5 How to calculate the FCF

Earnings before interest, taxes, depreciation and amortization (EBITDA)
− Depreciation and Amortization Expenses
= Earnings before interest and taxes (EBIT)
− Taxes on this EBIT
= Earnings before interest and after taxes (EBIaT)
+ Depreciation and amortization expenses
= FCF from operations
+/− Variations in the operational working capital = FCF from operational working capital
+/− Variations in capital expenditure = FCF from capital expenditure
= Total FCF

Table 2.5 shows how to calculate this FCF.

What Rate of Discount?

The FCF provides very important information about how a management decision can generate EV. Since the FCF comes from the assets, it reflects the generation of liquidity (real money) coming from the operational aspects of the management decision we want to analyze.

In the evaluation of a company, the FCF is the real money this company can generate as a consequence of the application (for good or bad) of all the operational policies. How the management team manages the operational aspects of a company is directly reflected in the FCF. And this FCF has nothing to do with how the company is financed.

If we use the FCF to estimate intrinsic EV creation, we have to discount it at a very specific rate.

This rate of discount is the WACC. This catches the expected minimum yield our providers of finance want to make, considering the risk, opportunity costs and inflation associated with the assets they are financing.

Table 2.6 summarizes how to calculate the WACC.

Table 2.6 The WACC

$WACC = Kd \times (1-t) \times (D/V) + Ke,I \times (E/V)$
Where:
Kd = Cost of debt
t = Effective tax rate
D = Economic value of debt
E = Economic value of equity
V = Enterprise value
Ke,I = Cost of equity

EV in Practice: The Useful Answers

As noted above, any management decision can be analyzed from different perspectives, taking into account different criteria and objectives. From a financial point of view, a management decision will only be sound if it helps the company to be economically feasible and profitable, and therefore to survive.

A company is economically feasible when it consistently generates enough FCF to pay back the amortization of the principal of the debt.

A company is economically profitable when it consistently generates enough FCF to pay back the service of the debt and to remunerate the shareholders properly.

Economic feasibility and profitability depend on the generation of enough FCF, but it also depends on a company's financial structure. In other words, if we want to create EV in a company we have to increase its generation of differential and sustainable FCF, but we also have to use an appropriate capital structure that makes the company feasible and minimizes the WACC.

Figure 2.1 summarizes the basic value drivers associated with any management decision or any economic valuation.

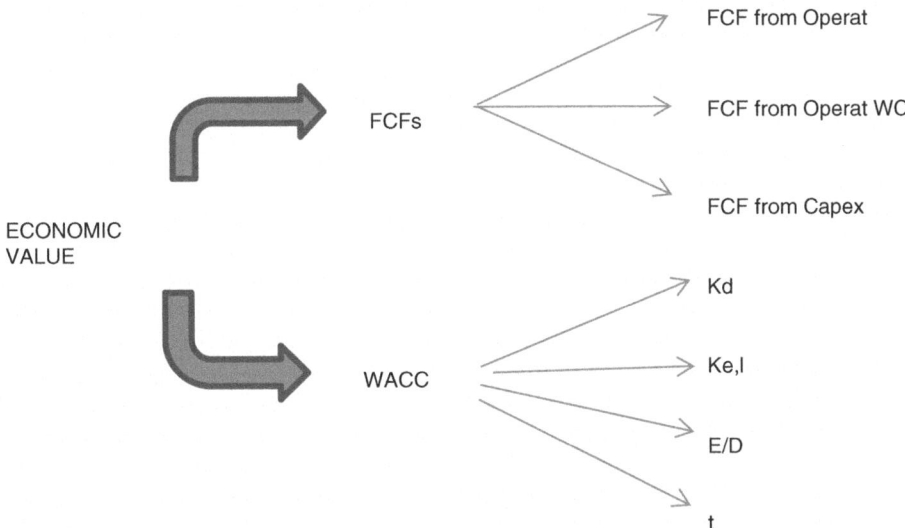

Fig. 2.1 Economic value and economic value drivers

Dealing with Risk

An important part of EV involves the consideration of risks associated with corporate decision-making that target the creation of value. In this sense, going too far is just as bad as coming up short.

Where are the risks in our valuation model that uses cash flows discounted at WACC?

In FCFs, we must consider the main operating risks inherent to the different business policies of the company involving sales, personnel, logistics, production, overheads, collection, investment, etc. Once these risks have been identified and their importance quantified, they are normally included in the valuation model through sensitivity analyses or probability simulations.

WACC includes financial risk stemming from the financial leverage ratio implied by the capital structure; risks perceived by shareholders, which form part of the cost of equity (market-risk premium and systematic operating and financial risks of the company); and risksperceived by financial entities that are included in the cost of debt.

Figure 2.2 summarizes these concepts.

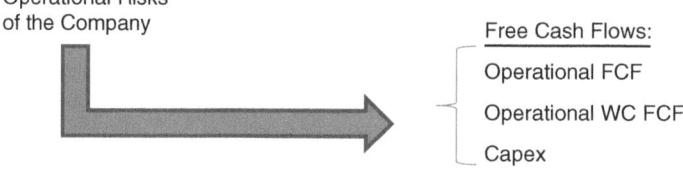

Operational Risks of the Company

Free Cash Flows:

Operational FCF

Operational WC FCF

Capex

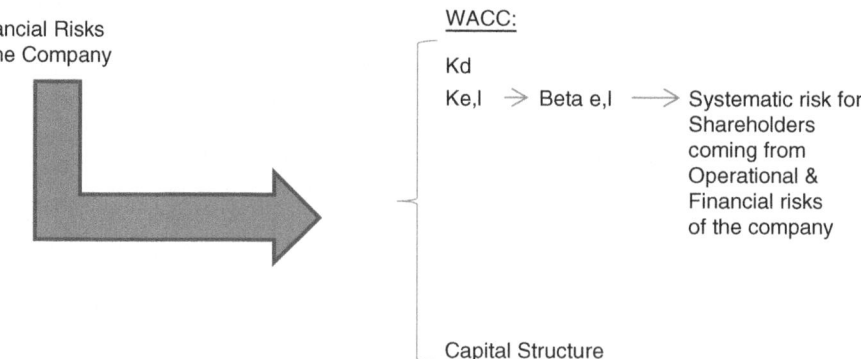

Financial Risks of the Company

WACC:

Kd

Ke,l → Beta e,l ⟶ Systematic risk for Shareholders coming from Operational & Financial risks of the company

Capital Structure

Fig. 2.2 Summary of risks in a company

Real Options to the Rescue?

In some cases, when operational flexibility is important, we should complete the EV by using a discounted cash flow (DCF) analysis: adding the eventual value associated with real options included in the decision. This could be the case with some investments that have a significant future expectations component which may or may not happen, but with a high value in case of success. In those cases, to properly evaluate the decision we should consider the value derived from having an option of being a player in case of future success.

If this is the case, the key point is not only whether we have an option, but mainly whether that option has a relevant value. This approach is not a magic formula to get a magical return from an unprofitable situation.

In other words, before delving into more or less esoteric calculations to evaluate options, it is desirable to clearly understand the following:

1. When there is a real option in a project.
   a. When there is a real possibility of altering the future when facing a change in circumstances; for example, by delaying a project, abandoning it or expanding it.
   b. When there is time before a decision has to be made on that future opportunity.
2. When a real option offers value.
   a. When it is possible to gain something by exercising the option. This only happens when there is something exclusive about the option being considered and when this opportunity exists during the period leading up to the making of the decision.

The result of this is that, before increasing the estimated EV of a decision (whether or not it is considered a strategic decision), through the value of an option, we should be sure that the option makes sense and, in particular, that it offers value. For example, it is clear that the EV of a project clouded by great uncertainty brought on by a future technological development will increase significantly if it is possible to wait and see what will happen regarding the technology. However, if the option of waiting is not exclusive, and everyone has the same option, it offers no value.

Additionally, valuation models of real options are borrowed from theoretical developments that have been conceived and applied to options involving future financial scenarios. What may be reasonable for a financial reality is not always reasonable for a non-financial reality. This means that the valuation model for real options is limited by a series of factors – as are all valuation models – that should be understood. The following are the main technical limitations stemming from the extrapolation to financial assets of valid valuation techniques:

1. The underlying asset is not necessarily traded in an organized public market.
2. The price of the underlying asset is not necessarily changing through an ongoing process.
3. The change taking place in the asset may not be known, and if it is, it may vary over time.
4. The exercising of the option may not be instantaneous.
5. The valuation of financial options is based on the existence of a parallel portfolio with cash flows that are identical to those of the option. This may not accurately reflect circumstances in the case of real options.

In summary, the valuation of real assets by extrapolating the theory of options involves a series of limitations where concept and application are concerned. This does not make the model useless, but, in certain cases it may give rise to doubts as to whether its use is reasonable.

Applying EV to Digital Business

In Chapter 1 we analyzed the main characteristics of digital business and digital transformation in a company. Whether the management decisions involved in these processes will create or destroy EV depends on whether these new opportunities and situations are able to generate the required FCF, financed via the appropriate capital structure, to produce a positive present value.

Let's analyze some examples from this perspective.

Paying for the New Users

In digital business, it's relatively frequent to justify an investment because of the number of new users resulting from the decision.

For example, let's assume that company A pays $10 billion for company B because company B has 300 million users. This operation implies a ratio EV to users of $33.33 per user.

How can we know if this value makes sense?

One way is to see what the market is paying for similar transactions with similar characteristics. Let's assume we are able to get this information, and the market is paying $25 per user. Accordingly, we can say that we are paying a premium of 33% in terms of extrinsic EV.[2]

In terms of intrinsic EV, if company A pays that amount for company B it is because A believes that B is worth more than the $10 billion. Otherwise, all the EV of B would go to the sellers, the owners of company B before the transaction.

Knowing whether paying the $10 billion for company B makes sense or not depends on understanding how B makes money; in other words, how B is able to generate positive FCF based on its business model. The increase in the number of users can be monetized via different routes.

Let's assume that company B generates revenue in three ways:

1. Instead of charging its basic users, B sells advertising to businesses interested in reaching the users of B.
2. B offers enhanced services to basic users.
3. B tries to sell data from these users to businesses interested in knowing about their behavior.

Once more, if company A pays $10 billion for company B it is because A thinks that B's business model will generate, using these methods, enough FCF to compensate for the price.

Let's assume that in the negotiation process, both parties agree on the window about the maximum and minimum EV of company B.

1. Minimum value: the EV of company B if it continues, standing alone. Let's assume it is estimated to be $6 billion.
2. Maximum price: the EV of company B operated by company A, including synergies. Let's assume this is estimated to be $16 billion.

In this case, we can agree that the estimated EV of the synergies in this operation is $10 billion (= 16 − 6). With an agreed price of $10 billion, it's clear that these synergies have been broken down into two parts: $6 billion for the buyer and $4 billion for the seller.

Assuming these are the facts, the question still remains about whether to pay $10 billion for company B makes sense.

---

[2] To get information about market value of current multiples in digital companies, visit www.petsky prunier.com.

Extrinsic value tells us that we are paying a premium of 33%.

Intrinsic value gives us more information. As mentioned above, we paid $10 billion because we estimated an EV of $16 billion. This means that new users coming from this operation will generate differential and sustainable FCFs for company A at a level that, discounted at a reasonable WACC, will produce a present value (PV) of $16 billion.

So, we have to be convinced that these 300 million of users of company B:

1. Are really new and differential users for company A.
2. Will generate differential FCFs for company A.
3. Will generate sustainable FCFs for company A.
4. Will generate FCFs in an amount that, discounted at the WACC of company A, will generate a PV of $16 billion.

Note what this means:

1. We have to consider only differential, new, incremental users to company A coming from company B. Shared users are not differential, unless we can offer them new services and generate new cash flows to A because of the acquisition of B.
2. These incremental users have to generate sustainable cash flows, which mean that these users will remain in A forever, regardless of the actions of the competition.

This is a crucial point for understanding any valuation in digital business, and whether it is reasonable or not. In practical terms, this means that the users of company B have to be incremental and active. Registered and passive users are good, but not good enough.[3]

Developing this operation with a more detailed numerical example will help to clarify the economic significance of these points, and this is shown in Table 2.7.

Assuming a reasonable WACC for company A of 8%, annual increases of 10% in the FCF during the next five years, and a TV in Year 5 equivalent to the value of a perpetuity of the average FCF for these five years, growing at 3%, the initial incremental FCF to company A coming from company B should be $0.73 billion.

---

[3] Applying this outlook we can understand better some recent doubts about valuations made by companies such as Twitter and Facebook.

Table 2.7 An economic analysis of the operation

Years		1	2	3	4	5
FCF		0.73	0.80	0.88	0.97	1.07
TV						18.36
Total FCF		0.73	0.80	0.88	0.97	19.43
WACC	8.0%					
PV	16.00					
TV	18.36					
FCFb	0.89					
growth rate	3.0%					
WACC	8.0%					
# users	300	330	363	399	439	483
EV/# users						
Buying at	33.33	$/per user				
Selling at	38.00	$/per user				

Figures in US$ billion

Table 2.8 A summary of the operation

Facts:
A buys B at a EV of $10 billion
B has 300 million users
A is valuing B at $33.33 per user

Assumptions:
A believes that B worth $16 billion
Assuming that A has a WACC of 8% and that is a reasonable WACC to be used for this operation,

Economic analysis:
It will make sense to evaluate B at $16 billion only if:
1. the first and differential FCF coming from this acquisition is $0.73 billion
2. FCFs for next five years will grow at 10% annually
3. the EV of B in five years will be $18.36 billion
This TV of $18.36 billion is equivalent to:
1. the value of a perpetuity of the average FCF during this five years, growing at 3%
2. to evaluate B in Year 5 at $38 per user, assuming A will keep all the users and that they will grow at 10% every year.

The TV needed in five years can also be compared with the price we are paying now in terms of dollars per user. If we now pay $33.33 per user, we have to be convinced that in five years we'll be able to sell the company at $38 per user, assuming we keep all the users and that they remain differential and growing at 10% every year.

Table 2.8 summarizes the economic consequences associated with the acquisition of company B by company A, at a price of $10 billion.

Based on this analysis about expected FCFs, we now have elements in place through which we can judge whether this operation, at this price, makes sense. We should ask ourselves:

1. What is the present FCF generated in company B for these 300 million users?
2. How many of these users will be new and differential for company A?
3. What are the actions company A is going to implement in company B to make possible that the differential users for A will generate a FCF of $0.73 billion in the first year?
4. What are the actions company A is going to implement in company B in the coming five years to maintain these differential users and to grow at 10% every year?

What About Financing?

To understand the economic consequences of paying $10 billion for company B we have to understand how reasonable its expected EV is. This EV depends not only on the expected FCFs, but also on how the operation will be financed and, consequently, on the expected WACC.

We have assumed that a reasonable WACC for this operation is 8%. It's time to explain why.

Let's consider that company B before the operation has a very conservative capital structure (no debt) and that one of the synergies company A sees in the acquisition of B comes from the expected EV that A can generate in B by changing its capital structure.

Let's assume that the expected future capital structure associated with company B acquired by company A would have a financial leverage of 30%. In this case, the relevant WACC to discount the differential FCFs in order to evaluate B would be 8%, because we assume a cost of equity (Ke,l) of 9%, a cost of debt (Kd) of 6% and an effective tax rate (t) of 15%. See Table 2.9.

Note that the acquisition of company B should be financed in a way that is consistent with the expected future capital structure associated with the new company A (30% debt/70% equity, 30D/70E).

Table 2.9 Estimation of WACC

Capital structure =30D/70E
Ke,l = 9%
Kd = 6%
t = 15%
WACC = 8%

For example, company A can decide to pay this $10 billion in cash and to finance this payment with an amount of debt that makes the capital structure of the new A equal to that expected (30D/70E). In that case, we can easily assume that this way of financing is consistent with the valuation.

But, alternatively, company A may decide to pay this $10 billion in cash ($4 billion), using cash in excess and the rest ($6 billion) in shares of A. In this case, the acquisition will be financed through equity alone, and we have to know how the capital structure of the new A (present A + future B operated by A) would change to a 30D/70E, as expected.

What About the Distribution of the EV?

In summary, how the operation is financed can affect the expected EV of the operation and the distribution of this EV.

Why? Because:

1. The acquisition of company B should be financed in a way that is consistent with the expected future capital structure associated with the new company A (30D/70E).
2. If company A pays the shareholders of company B in shares of A, it is relevant how the exchange rate between one share of A and one share of B is determined.

For example, if company A pays the shareholders of company B by valuing a share of A as equal to a share of B, we have to be convinced that the estimated prices are equal. Otherwise, this exchange rate will be unfair and will destroy value for the present shareholders, creating value for the other shareholders. Table 2.10 shows some examples.

Table 2.10 Comparison of alternatives

Estimated exchange rate: 1 share of A = 1 share of B			
Estimated equity of B	10,000		
# shares of B	1,000		
Price of share of B	10		

Assuming an exchange rate of 1 share of A = 1 share of B			
Alternatives	1	2	3
Estimated equity of A	50,000	80,000	40,000
# of shares of A	5,000	5,000	5,000
Price of share of A	10	16	8
Comments	Fair agreement	Value transfer to B	Value transfer to A

Connecting Extrinsic and Intrinsic EV

So far we have defined two ways in which to measure EV: extrinsic (market based) and intrinsic (business model based). As noted, these two approaches are complementary ways in which a (hopefully) reasonable opinion about EV can be given. But how are these two values related? When can we say that a comparable value originating from the market is supported by an intrinsic EV based on a reasonable business model?

Common sense tells us that in the long term everyone will pay more for a company if it is likely to produce better returns. Nobody invests his/her money in order to lose it. From an investor´s perspective, therefore, any extrinsic value should be explained in terms of its associated FCF estimated in PV.

For mature and relatively low capital intensive industries, the operational earnings of a company can be considered a good proxy for its FCF. Since FCF has three components, assuming the operational working capital (OWC) component is close to zero, and that the company needs a capital expenditure equal to the depreciation and amortization expenses, then FCF can be considered very close to the earnings before interests and after taxes (EBIaT), a typical measure of net (after taxes) operational earnings (without interest expenses).

In these cases, the expected generation of EBIaT of the company is a good proxy for the expected generation of FCF, and any comparison with EV/EBIaT can be easily related to the FCF needed to justify the valuation.

When the company operates in an industry which is neither mature nor low capital intensive, we have to consider the investments in OWC and capital expenditure that any business needs to survive. This is the case for most digital businesses.

Dealing with innovation

To cope with the digital revolution, innovation is needed more than ever. Companies need to constantly innovate to keep pace with ever-changing consumer demand. New product and service innovations can be categorized in three levels of innovation:

1. Sustaining Innovation. Also called incremental innovation, it represents small, yet significant improvements or upgrades to add or sustain value to existing products, services and processes. Examples include a

new version of a smartphone, new flavours, packaging improvements, and just-in-time or lean supply chain improvements. Most companies use incremental innovation to improve an existing product's development efficiency, productivity, competitive differentiation, and to help maintain or improve a product's market position.

2. Breakthrough Innovation. These are innovations that give consumers something unique or state-of-the-art technological advantage. This innovation creates a significant competitive advantage for a while, but in a world of increasingly global competition, the advantage period is becoming shorter which requires constant breakthrough Innovation. For example, Breakthrough innovations harnessing a new technology include the first ipod, the first iphone or Dyson, the world's first bagless vacuum cleaner. Examples of Breakthrough innovations harnessing a new business model include Microsoft office 365, InnoCentice crowdsourcing model and Zipcar business model.

3. Radical Innovation. Also called disruptive or transformational innovation, it is an invention or change that has not been seen before that creates a new industry and transforms our society and life. This kind of innovation disrupts the current markets, transforms the value proposition and often eliminates existing industries or, at a minimum, totally transforms them. It involves harnessing new technology and a new business model simultaneously and as such, radical innovation is very rare. When successfully accomplished, radical innovation typically provides vast benefits for society and business world. However, it also comes with a high degree of risk of resistance and failure. Examples include the telephone, automobile, television, microprocessor, Internet etc.

We can summarize these types of innovation as follows:

In sustaining/incremental innovation, we are dealing with an existing technology and an existing market, and the emphasis is put in the development of new products and services.

In breakthrough innovation, we focus in new markets for some given technology and products/services. In radical/disruptive innovation, we look for new technologies, new markets and the development of new products and services. Figure 2.3 shows a graphical representation of these types of innovation, in relation to market and products/services development.

The classification of the company's new product and services developments, within the framework of sustaining, breakout, or disruptive, allows a

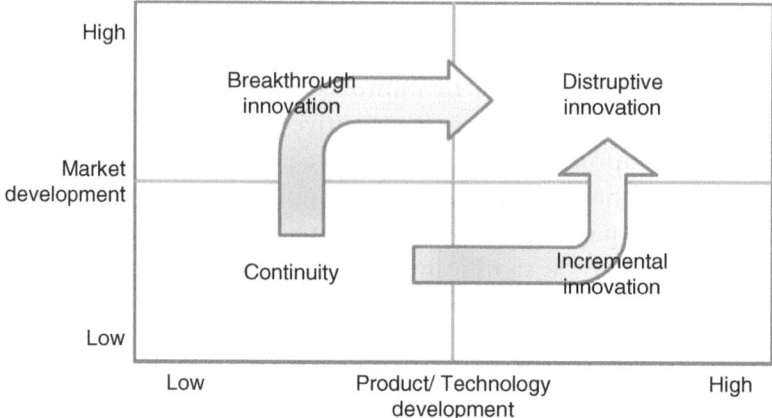

Fig. 2.3 Innovations and Business Ideas

company to develop an effective innovation portfolio by managing risks and rewards. Briefly, the typical revenue profile is:

- Sustaining: Immediately moderate, then its effects rapidly disappear.
- Breakthrough: Rapidly strong, then quickly dropping to a lower level.
- Radical: Longer gestation period leading to exponential growth.

Innovation and Economic Value

Like any other economic model, the intrinsic approach to estimate the economic value does have limits. When we use the traditional DCF approach to estimate the economic value we are assuming a very inflexible operational future, both in expected amounts and in timing. Expected FCF will occur in a deterministic future, in a given amount and in a given moment.

This lack of operational flexibility in the traditional DCF approach can lead to an underestimation of the economic value associated to some investments, especially when a business model is based on an effective management of future risks and rewards based on innovation. This is what happens in a digital world.

The higher the importance of innovation to become a survivor, the higher the importance of operational flexibility to create economic value. As previously commented, we can introduce the value of this operational flexibility in our traditional DCF approach in different ways:Setting up different

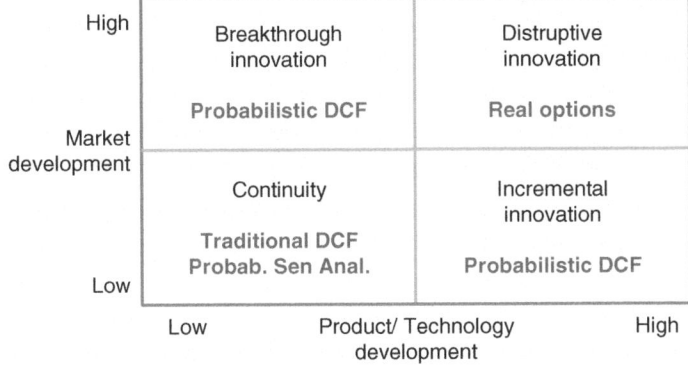

Fig. 2.4 Innovations, Business Ideas and Valuation

scenarios with different probabilities (probabilistic sensitivity analysis). Transforming some of the variables from deterministic to probabilistic, and estimating a probabilistic economic value based on simulations.

Introducing the economic value of some real options associated to the business model. Figure 2.4 shows the link between these valuation approaches and the innovation associated to different business models.

From Traditional Value Metrics to Digital Value Metrics

It is obvious that there are some advantages in using only a simple metric (number of users, for example) to justify an investment decision. Among other benefits, it is simple, clear and understandable. And, providing the market is signaling a reasonable EV, it provides a useful price.

The problem is that the extrinsic EV is not always reasonable and, consequently, it is very convenient to understand it in terms of the implicit assumptions that are made regarding the key value drivers associated with its intrinsic EV, as explained above.

Additionally, to create EV we have to select the right alternative but we also have to implement it. And this implementation can become impossible when the people responsible do not fully understand the underlying assumptions that are implicit in the expected EV to be created, or when these assumptions are not realistic and/or reasonable.

Keeping these comments in mind, we can conclude that any value metric is a shortcut to analyze EV, and that it can be very useful to establish and

Table 2.11 Some value metrics

Acquisition of B for A						
Some value metrics						
Years	Now	1	2	3	4	5
Estimated new users (in million)	300	330	363	399	439	483
Expected FCFs (in $ million)		730	803	883	972	1,069
Expected FCF per user (in $ million)		2.21	2.21	2.21	2.21	2.21
Economic value per user (in $)	33.33					38.00

communicate management's objectives for the implementation of any value-based management approach.

In any case, the key point is not what value metric we use (digital oriented or not), but whether the quantification of that value metric is consistent with the general objective of EV creation.

Going back to the example developed in the previous section, we can explain a price of $10 billion for company B based on different metrics, such as users, revenue and expected TV, but we have to realize that the explanation of that price is not based on just one metric, and that the expected evolution of any metric must be consistent with the analysis of the reasonable intrinsic EV. Table 2.11 provides an example of how to link a value metric (number of users) with the expected EV in the acquisition of company B by company A at a price of $10 billion.

In summary, to justify the acquisition of company B at a price of $10 billion in terms of number of users, we have to be convinced not only that company A is getting 300 million new users for that acquisition, but also that:

1. These differential users will remain and will grow at 10% every year, adding up to a differential FCF of $2.21 per user every year.
2. The EV per user in five years will be $38 per user.

Of course, a similar analysis can be done for any metric we want to use. In Table 2.12 we see a summary of some of the most frequently used value metrics, including operational metrics related to digital business.

Regarding the relationship between value metrics and the measure of EV, we can establish the following conclusions:

1. Most of the metrics do not measure the value created by a business decision correctly, as they refer to data for just one year, when business decisions create value over the whole period in which they take place.

Table 2.12 A summary of value metrics

1. Accounting Metrics

Definition	Formula	What it measures
NOPAT	**EBIaT**	An accounting operating result

Where:
NOPAT = Net operating profit after taxes
EBIaT = Earnings before interest and after taxes

ROA	**NOPAT/TA**	Accounting yield on assets

Where:
ROA = Return on assets
TA = Total assets (at accounting value)

ROE	**NOPAT/TE**	Accounting yield for shareholders

Where:
ROE = Return on equity
TE = Total equity (at accounting value)

2. Cash flow metrics

Definition	Formula	What it measures
FCF from operations	**EBIaT + DE**	Cash coming from operations

Where:
FCF from operations = Free cash flow from operations
DE = Depreciation expenses
A Summary of Value Metrics

FCF f/OWC	**Variation in OWC**	Cash coming from OWC

Where:
FCF f/OWC = free cash flow from operational working capital
Variation in OWC = variations in operational working capital

FCF f/Capex	**Variation in gross FA**	Cash coming from Capex

Where:
FCF f/Capex = Free cash flow from investments in fixed assets
Variation in gross FA = Variations in gross fixed assets
Total FCF = FCF f/Operations + FCF f/OWC + FCF f/Capex
Total FCF = Total free cash flow
It measures the cash flow coming from the assets, independently of the financing.

3. Metrics based on Activity

Definition	Formula	What it measures
# Users	**Number of users**	**Traffic**
Revenue p/User	**T. Rev/#Users**	**Revenue per user**

Where:
T. Rev = Total revenue

(continued)

Table 2.12 (continued)

#Users = number of users		
NOPAT p/User	**NOPAT/#Users**	**NOPAT per user**
FCF p/User	**Total FCF/#Users**	**FCF per user**
EV p/User	**EV/#Users**	**EV per user**

Where:
EV = Enterprise value (economic value of total net assets)
A summary of value metrics
4. Metrics based on discounted cash flow

Definition	Formula	What it measures
EV	**PV of FCF**	**Intrinsic EV**

Where:
PV of FCF = Present value of FCF discounted at WACC

Equity value	**PV of ECF**	**Intrinsic economic value of equity**

Where:
PV of ECF = Present value of equity cash flows discounted at Ke,l
ECF = Equity cash flows (= FCF – total service of debt)

SVA	**Variation in equity value in two periods**	

Where:
SVA = Shareholder's value added

MVA	**Difference between equity at economic value and equity at accounting value in a given period.**	

Where:
MVA = Market value added
5. Metrics based on economic profitability

Definition	Formula	What it measures
IRR	**IRR of FCF**	**Economic yield of assets**

Where:
IRR = Internal rate of return

IRR of ECF	**IRR of ECF**	**Economic yield for shareholders**

2. When they are used as a measure of value created by the management of a company, it is necessary to bear in mind the conceptual limitations inherent in their formulation.
3. It is therefore necessary to know what a metric measures and to act accordingly.
4. The use of any value metric must be linked to business value generators, as a relative rather than absolute formulation that facilitates the achievement of partial objectives related to a general objective.

Metrics in Practice

As a practical example, let's analyze the acquisition of company B by company A in terms of some value metrics.

Remember that A is paying $10 billion for B. Let's assume that the accounting value of B is $5 billion.

Table 2.13 details the evolution of the FCFs.

With this additional information, we can calculate the expected evolution of some metrics, as follows:

1. Revenue per user = $30.30 per user
2. NOPAT per user = $3.86 per user
3. FCF per user = $2.21 $ per user
4. ROA = 25.50%
5. IRR of FCF = 19.88%

We can therefore complete the information about users by pointing out that, in terms of number of users, to justify the acquisition of company B at a price of $10 billion, we have to be convinced that not only is company A getting 300 million new users for that acquisition, but also that

1. These differential users will remain and will grow at 10% every year, adding differential revenue per user of $30.30 per user every year, differential net operating profit after tax per user of $3.86 per user every year, and differential FCF per user of $2.21 per user every year.
2. The EV per user in five years will be $38 per user.

Table 2.13 Expected evolution of FCF (detailed)

Years	1	2	3	4	5
Revenue	10.00	11.00	12.10	13.31	14.64
Operating costs & expenses	−8.00	−8.80	−9.68	−10.65	−11.71
EBITDA	2.00	2.20	2.42	2.66	2.93
DA	−0.50	−0.55	−0.61	−0.67	−0.73
EBIT	1.50	1.65	1.82	2.00	2.20
Taxes (15%)	−0.23	−0.25	−0.27	−0.30	−0.33
EBIaT (NOPAT)	1.28	1.40	1.54	1.70	1.87
DA	0.50	0.55	0.61	0.67	0.73
FCF f/Operating	1.78	1.95	2.15	2.36	2.60
FCF f/OWC	−0.50	−0.55	−0.61	−0.67	−0.73
FCF f/ capital expenditure	−0.55	−0.60	−0.66	−0.73	−0.80
Total FCF	0.73	0.80	0.88	0.97	1.07

This acquisition will produce an accounting profitability of 25.50%, but the economic profitability will be 19.88%.

Summary

1. EV is not just a qualitative value, as, for example, sentimental value is. A house may have considerable sentimental value but a very low EV.
2. EV is not just an accounting value. A company may have a strong accounting value, but a not so brilliant EV. Why? Because the accounting value deals with historical information, presented in an accurate, systematic and consistent way, while for the EV we also have to consider the expected future and the associated risks.
3. Any measure of EV must include an appropriate conceptual and practical response to three elements: the generation of real money (cash flows); the expected future of the business; the associated risks.
4. There are two ways in which to measure EV.
5. First, we have the extrinsic EV, which is an EV that comes from what the market considers. Extrinsic EV is certainly a reference to be considered, but it's not always the best way to get a reasonable EV.
6. That's why we have to complement extrinsic EV with the intrinsic EV. With this, we try to calculate the EV of something based on its accounting value and its future business plans. In other words, we do not take for granted that the price will naturally reflect this transition from accounting value to a reasonable EV.
7. To create EV in a digital business, and in any business for that matter, we have to generate enough differential and sustainable cash flows, so that discounted at the minimum expected economic profitability desired by our providers of financial resources (debt and equity), the PV would still be positive and better than the alternatives.
8. In digital business, it is relatively usual to justify an investment because of the new users resulting from the decision.
9. Before paying for new users, we have to understand how the business model of the digital company is able to generate revenue through these customers.
10. We have to realize that this means considering only differential, new, incremental users resulting from the decision. Shared users are not differential, unless we can offer them new services and generate new cash flows through the decision.

11. These incremental users have to generate sustainable cash flows, which means that they will remain in the company for ever, regardless the actions of the competition.
12. In practical terms, this means that we should consider only users who are incremental and active. Registered and passive users are good, but not good enough.
13. How a management decision is financed can affect the expected EV of that decision and the distribution of this EV.
14. To cope with the digital revolution, innovation is needed more than ever. Companies need to constantly innovate to keep pace with ever-changing consumer demand.
15. New product and service innovations can be categorized in three levels of innovation: Sustaining, Breakthrough and Radical.
16. The higher the importance of innovation to become a survivor, the higher the importance of operational flexibility to create economic value. We can introduce the value of this operational flexibility in our traditional DCF approach in different ways: probabilistic sensitivity analysis; transforming some of the variables from deterministic to probabilistic, and estimating a probabilistic economic value based on simulations; and introducing the economic value of some real options associated to the business model.
17. Any value metric is a shortcut to analyse economic value and it can be very useful to establish and communicate management objectives for the implementation of any value-based management approach.
18. In any case, the key point is not what value metric we use (digital oriented or not), but whether the quantification of that value metric is consistent with the more general objective of economic value creation.

3

Escaping the Hype: Dealing With Subjectivity and Finding the Right Price

Introduction

When dealing with valuation, the key question is very clear. It can be formulated as follows:

What Is the Value of This?

By *value* we mean economic value (EV), not other kinds, such as sentimental value or accounting value.

By *this* we normally mean assets, and we mean any kind of assets: tangible, material assets, such as warehouses, machines, buildings, stores; intangible, non-material assets, such as goodwill, patents, brands; financial assets, such as a minority participation in a company or a bond issued by the government.

In Chapter 2 we discussed what EV is and how we can measure it. In this chapter we are going to focus on how to determine the value of a digital company, how to evaluate the assets (tangible, intangible, financial) that form a company (or a set of companies) operating in, or related to, digital business.

Valuation: Dealing with Subjectivity

When we evaluate a company we want to have a reasonable idea of how much we would pay for it, considering its EV. This means that any valuation is an opinion and, like any opinion, it can be anything from a very reasonable judgment to an absolutely ridiculous notion.

© The Author(s) 2017
F.J. López Lubián, J. Esteves, *Value in a Digital World*,
DOI 10.1007/978-3-319-51750-6_3

How do we avoid ridiculous notions and achieve reasonable judgments? By bringing focus to the valuation we want to make. To do this we have to understand the following:

1. What we want to evaluate.
2. The reason we want to evaluate a company: value for what purpose?
3. From what perspective we want to evaluate a company: value for whom?
4. Under what circumstances we want to evaluate a company.

For example, if we want to evaluate a digital company, such as Google, first of all we have to focus the valuation:

1. Which Google do we want to evaluate? The one coming from the past, or a new Google based on future projects?
2. Assuming we want to evaluate Google based on its future, we have to decide its value for what. In the context of a possible merger and acquisition (M&A)? To estimate the value of a minority shareholder for an eventual initial public offering (IPO)?
3. Having decided on the Google we want to evaluate (future Google in the context of a possible M&A with another company, for example), now we have to determine the value for whom. Value from the seller's perspective? Value from the buyer's perspective? Value from the perspective of a third party that is also interested in an eventual acquisition?
4. Finally, keeping in mind the above points, we have to consider the circumstances, both internal and external, under which we are making the valuation. Is the economy in a huge recession? Is the industry booming? Are the sellers in a hurry to complete?

In some cases, circumstances can be a decisive factor influencing the valuation. For example, the timing of the operation is crucial, as these cases make clear:

1. In 1999 Yahoo had the opportunity to buy Google, then a start-up, for less than $1 million.
2. Telefónica bought Tuenti in August 2010, when the aim was that Tuenti would become the Spanish alternative to Facebook.
3. In 2013, Facebook offered $3 billion for WhatsApp. One year later, the acquisition took place for $19 billion.

After focusing on the valuation, we can deduce the reasonable EV of a company using an extrinsic and an intrinsic approach. These approaches are complementary and related, as discussed in Chapter 2.

How can we know if the extrinsic EV is reasonable? By being convinced that the capital market is not over/under valued (for public companies), or that we are using information of companies, multiples and transactions which are comparable with the company we want to evaluate (in the case of private companies). To judge how reasonable any comparison is we first have to focus the valuation.

Whether or not an intrinsic EV is reasonable is related to the assumptions we make on the expected free cash flow (FCF) and on the weighted average cost of capital (WACC), to get a reasonable EV. Note that to judge whether any assumption is reasonable, we also need to focus the valuation.

Valuation in a Digital World

Between 2012 and 2015 the total value of startup tech firms valued at $1 billion-plus (so-called "unicorns": tech firms which have yet to come to the stock market but are valued at $1 billion-plus) went from $100 billion to $505 billion. For example, Zenefits (software) raised money in May 2015 with a $4.5 billion valuation.

But in late 2015, several mutual funds marked down the value of some of their holdings on these "unicorns." For example, Fidelity wrote down Dropbox (cloud storage firm) by 20%; Snapchat (messaging app) by 25% and Zenefits and Mongo DB (databases) by 50% each.

What's going on in this industry? Are we experiencing a financial bubble similar to the one we had at the beginning of this century? Is the market overreacting to an unlimited optimism about the expected growth targets of these companies? Are they being valued as if they were guaranteed to be among the long-term winners in their line of business when, in fact, not all can survive?

In situations like this, where many of the most valuable startups come from the digital world (see Fig. 3.1), it's very important to understand the sustainability of the business model associated with a particular valuation.

An example of how to apply valuation methodology to a tech firm will help us to discuss and clarify these issues.

Valuation of the 10 most valuable venture-backed private companies*

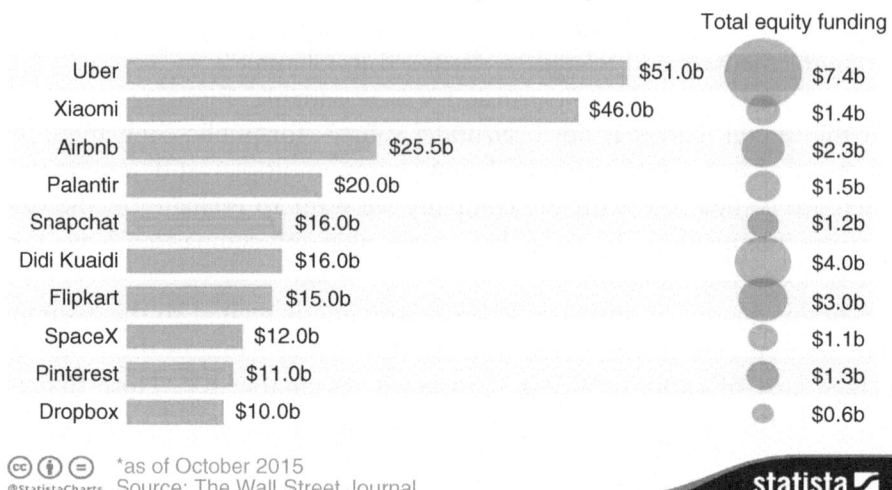

Total equity funding

Uber	$51.0b	$7.4b
Xiaomi	$46.0b	$1.4b
Airbnb	$25.5b	$2.3b
Palantir	$20.0b	$1.5b
Snapchat	$16.0b	$1.2b
Didi Kuaidi	$16.0b	$4.0b
Flipkart	$15.0b	$3.0b
SpaceX	$12.0b	$1.1b
Pinterest	$11.0b	$1.3b
Dropbox	$10.0b	$0.6b

*as of October 2015
@StatistaCharts Source: The Wall Street Journal

statista ⚡

Fig. 3.1 The world's most valuable startups

Valuation of Tech.com

Let's assume that we want to evaluate Tech.com, a digital company operating in robotics.

To do this, we have to focus on the valuation.

Which Tech.com (TCH) do we want to evaluate? Let's assume that we want to estimate a reasonable EV of TCH based on its future, in the context of a possible acquisition of TCH by a competitor (CCM). And we want to estimate a reasonable maximum value that TCH might have for the buyer, assuming CCM takes over and implements all the synergies that are possible.

Let's assume the valuation takes place at the end of 2016, and use information based on that date. The balance sheet (BS) statement of TCH is the following:

Evaluating Tech.com			
Figures in million Euros			
Balance sheet			
Net current assets	10.0	debt	10.0
Net fixed assets	80.0	equity	80.0
Total net assets	90.0	debt + equity	90.0

With this information, the EV of TCH at accounting value is €90 million, and the accounting value of the equity is €80 million. Since the number of shares of TCH is 80 million, the accounting value per share is €1.

We want to discuss how we can estimate a reasonable maximum EV of TCH, in the context of an eventual acquisition.

Since TCH is a private company, an extrinsic reference to its EV can be what the market is paying for similar companies in similar operations. Let's assume that the market is paying an EV equal to 15 times the number of users. Since TCH has 50 million users, an estimated EV would be €750 million.

The profit and loss (P&L) statement of TCH for 2016 is the following:

P&L statement Figures in million Euros	
Year	2016
Revenue	100.0
Cost of sales	−40.0
Gross margin	60.0
Operational expenses	−30.0
Earnings before interest, taxes, depreciation and amortization (EBITDA)	30.0
DA	−5.0
Earnings before interest and taxes (EBIT)	25.0
Taxes on EBIT (25%)	−6.3
Earnings before interest and after taxes (EBIaT)	18.8
FCF from operations	23.8

If we accept an EV of €750 million, we are paying:

- EV/users = 15 Euros per user
- EV/revenue = 7.5 times
- EV/EBITDA = 25 times

Does it make sense to pay €750 million for something with an accounting value of €90 million? Or to pay €15 per user, 7.5 times the revenue and 25 times the EBITDA? To answer these questions we need to analyze an estimated intrinsic value of the TCH we have already defined.

The Expected business Plan of TCH Operated by CCM

Let's assume that a reasonable business plan of the future TCH, operated by CCM and including all the synergies, can be summarized as in Table 3.1.

In this business plan we can see the expected synergies that CCM will implement, summarized in an major increase in new users, a reduction in operational expenses from 30% of revenue to 25% in five years, and a better management of operational working capital (OWC), reflected in a decrease to 15 days of revenue, down from the present 36 days. Prices will increase by 3% every year.

Table 3.1 Expected FCF

Years	Now	1	2	3	4	5	Assumptions
New users	50.0	57.5	69.0	82.8	99.4	124.2	
Annual growth		15%	20%	20%	20%	25%	
Revenue/users	2.0	2.1	2.1	2.2	2.3	2.3	3% increase
Expected revenue		118.5	146.4	181.0	223.7	288.0	
Cost of sales		−47.4	−58.6	−72.4	−89.5	−115.2	40% of revenue
Gross margin		71.1	87.8	108.6	134.2	172.8	
Operational expenses		−35.5	−19.3	−21.5	−24.8	−31.1	30/28/26/25/25 of revenue
EBITDA		35.5	68.5	87.0	109.4	141.7	
DA		−5.9	−7.3	−9.0	−11.2	−14.4	5% of revenue
EBIT		29.6	61.2	78.0	98.2	127.3	
Taxes on EBIT (25%)		−7.4	−15.3	−19.5	−24.5	−31.8	
EBIaT		22.2	45.9	58.5	73.6	95.5	
FCF from operations		28.1	53.2	67.5	84.8	109.9	
Evolution of Net Current Assets (NCA)							
Days of revenue	36	36	17	16	15	15	
Net Current Assets (NCA)	10.0	11.8	6.9	8.0	9.3	12.0	
FCF OWC		−1.8	4.9	−1.1	−1.3	−2.7	
Capital expenditure							
Maintenance		−5.9	−7.3	−9.0	−11.2	−14.4	Depreciation expenses
New investments		−17.8	−22.0	−27.1	−33.5	−43.2	15% of revenue
FCF capital expenditure		−23.7	−29.3	−36.2	−44.7	−57.6	
Total FCF		2.6	28.9	30.2	38.8	49.6	

Table 3.2 Alternative differential users

Years	Now	1	2	3	4	5
New users	35.0	38.5	43.1	48.4	55.7	64.1
Annual growth		10%	12%	12%	15%	15%

Since the expected generation of differential FCFs comes from the new users, a key factor is to be sure that all these new users will be differential and sustainable for CCM. In other words, we have to consider only the new users that CCM will have as a consequence of buying TCH. And in the next five years we have to include the new users that will remain with CCM, as noted in Chapter 2.

Once more, an example will help to clarify this point.

In Table 3.1 we are assuming that all the 50 million users of TCH will be new for CCM. And that, regardless the action of the competitors, in the future CCM will be able to increase this initial number with an annual growth of 15% in the first year, 20% in the second year and so on. What happens if only 70% of these 50 million users coming from TCH are new to CCM? And if, additionally, we believe that the net increase in new users in the following years will be lower owing to the expected actions of CCM's competitors? In this case, the number of users to be considered will be lower, as summarized in Table 3.2.

Alternative Ways to Monetize Users

Taking a more detailed approach, we can link the expected evolution of users with regard to revenue by analyzing the different ways in which the company can generate revenue according to its business model; in other words, not only by increasing the number of users, but by changing the mix of sources of revenue associated with these new users.

In Table 3.3 we can discover an alternative way in which to generate the expected revenue of TCH operated by CCM, with fewer users.

We can see that identifying the sources of revenue (advertising, premium services and sale of data), and their expected contribution to future revenue, we can get the same total revenue with a change in the number of users from 50 to 75 million, instead of 50 to 124.2 million.

Table 3.3 Detailed forecast of revenue

	Now	1	2	3	4	5	
Users Detailed	50.0	55.0	60.0	65.0	70.0	75.0	in million
In volume							
Advertising	90.0%	88.0%	82.0%	75.0%	70.0%	60.0%	
Premium services	7.0%	7.0%	10.0%	10.0%	10.0%	10.0%	
Data sold	3.0%	5.0%	8.0%	15.0%	20.0%	30.0%	
	100.0%	100.0%	100.0%	100.0%	100.0%	100.0%	
In pricing							
Advertising	1.82	1.88	1.93	1.99	2.20	2.28	$ per user
Premium services	3.00	3.09	3.58	3.60	3.71	3.80	$ per user
Data sold	5.00	5.75	6.21	6.21	6.43	6.62	$ per user
Contribution to revenue							
Advertising	82.0	90.8	95.1	97.1	107.8	102.6	in million
Premium services	10.5	11.9	21.5	23.4	26.0	28.5	in million
Data sold	7.5	15.8	29.8	60.5	90.0	148.9	in million
Total revenue	100.0	118.5	146.4	181.0	223.7	280.0	in million

Instead of number of users, can be based on the mix.

Dealing with Capital Structure

In terms of capital structure, the new TCH operated by CCM will be more financially leveraged, with an estimated capital structure of 30% debt/70% equity (30D/70E). As a consequence, the WACC for the new TCH will be 8.0%, as detailed in Table 3.4.

In Year 5 we can estimate a Terminal Value (TV, defined as the expected reasonable EV in Year 5) calculating the value of a perpetuity, growing at 3% and taking the FCF of Year 5 as the base FCF. This TV will be:

$$TV = FCF (1 + g)/(WACC - g) = €1{,}024.5 \text{ million [where g is growth rate]}$$

The present value (PV) of the expected FCF, including the TV, discounted at the WACC, is €811.3 million. This amount is the expected maximum EV of TCH operated by CCM. Note that the associated maximum equity will be €801.3 million.

In terms of price per share, if we pay €740 million for the equity of THC, we will be paying €9.25 per share, for a company with a maximum estimated value per share of €10.02 and an accounting value per share of €1.00.

Table 3.4 Expected WACC

Kd	5.0%
Ke,l	9.8%
T	25.0%
Kd (1-t)	3.8%
D	30.0%
Equity	70.0%
WACC	8.0%

Kd = Cost of debt.
Ke,l = Cost of Equity leveraged.
T = Marginal tax rate.
Kd (1-t) = Coste of debt after Taxes.
D = Debt.
WACC = Weigthed Average Cost of Capital.

We can summarize the situation as follows:

1. TCH has a present accounting value per share of €1.
2. If CCM accepts to pay the estimated extrinsic value of €15 per user, CCM will pay €9.25 per share.
3. Assuming all the users of TCH will be differential and sustainable for CCM and that CCM will successfully implement the expected synergies in TCH, the maximum price per share of TCH will be €10.02.

According to this, it seems that the buyer will pay too much for TCH if it pays the estimated extrinsic value of €15 per user, since it will pay a final price very close to the maximum one.

In any case, we can estimate the expected economic profitability for the shareholder of CCM if the company pays €9.25 for something with an estimated maximum value of €10.02. This profitability will be the expected internal rate of return (IRR) of the expected FCF for the shareholders.[1]

The IRR is 12.5%, as shown in Table 3.5. This confirms our previous estimate of the overvalued price if the buyer pays €9.25 per share.

Understanding the Terminal Value (TV)

In any intrinsic valuation using the discounted cash flow (DCF) methodology, a key element in the final EV comes from the TV.

How can we know whether the TV is reasonable?

First of all, we have to understand what TV is. In the TV we want to include our best estimation of the EV the company will have in the last year

Table 3.5 Capital structure

Evolution of capital structure						
Years		1	2	3	4	5
Equity	567.9	611.4	640.0	670.0	696.3	717.2
Debt	243.4	262.0	274.3	287.1	298.4	307.4
Valuation	811.3	873.4	914.3	957.1	994.7	1,024.5
WACC	8%	8%	8%	8%	8%	8%
FCF		2.6	28.9	30.2	38.8	49.6
Financial Expenses (1-t)		−9.1	−9.8	−10.3	−10.8	−11.2
Amortization of debt		18.7	12.3	12.8	11.3	8.9
FCF to shareholders		12.1	31.3	32.8	39.3	47.4
TV						717.2
Total FCF to shareholders		12.1	31.3	32.8	39.3	764.5
PV of FCF to shareholders	567.9					
Expected FCF shareholders						
They pay	506.6					
Years		1	2	3	4	5
FCF shareholders	−506.6	12.1	31.3	32.8	39.3	764.5
IRR	12.5%					

of our time horizon. In other words, we have to include as TV the value we believe we'll be able to sell the company in that last year.

Like any EV, this TV can be estimated following an intrinsic or an extrinsic approach. For example, in the valuation of TCH we are assuming that:

We will pay now	We will sell the company in five years
EV/users = 15.00	EV/users = 8.26
EV/revenue = 7.50	EV/revenue = 3.56
EV/ EBITDA = 25.00	EV/ EBITDA = 7.23

This is an interesting comparison, since it shows us that something must be wrong.

Why? Because it doesn't make too much sense to assume that, after implementing some important synergies in TCH over five years, the company will have an estimated extrinsic EV around 50% lower than the present one. Either we are paying too much for the present extrinsic EV, or we are undervaluing the future TV in terms of extrinsic EV.

Since we have already explained how we estimated the TV, let's now understand what is behind the present EV of €750 million, which we have estimated with an extrinsic approach.

Like any TV, this €750 million can be understood in terms of the value of an FCF in perpetuity, growing at a certain growth rate and using a base FCF.

Table 3.6 EV of 750 in terms of perpetuity

EV of 750 in terms of a perpetuity In 2016	
FCF from operations	23.8
FCF from OWC	−1.0
FCF from capital expenditure	−20.0
Total FCF	2.8
g	7.4%
WACC	7.8%
TV	750

If we use as a base FCF that of 2016, knowing that the WACC of TCH before this operation is 7.8% (reflecting a capital structure of 15D/ 85E, with a cost of equity (Ke,l) of 8.5%), we can estimate the needed growth rate to obtain a TV of €750 million, as shown in Table 3.6.

This analysis reflects a very clear conclusion: to pay €740 million for the equity of TCH will only make sense if CCM believes it will be able to make the present FCF of TCH grow forever at an annual compound rate higher than 7.4%.

Unless CCM, as a buyer, has a hidden agenda, the chances are that this market price of €15 per user is reflecting an overvaluation of TCH. Even in the best scenario (assuming that all the new users are differential and sustainable, and that the synergies will be operational and fully implemented), the expected economic profitability for CCM's shareholders will be only 12.5%.

At this point it's important to realize that the expected economic profitability for CCM's shareholders will depend, among other factors, on how much CCM will pay for TCH now. Don't confuse economic profitability with accounting profitability. In Table 3.7 we can see the expected evolution of the financial statements of the new TCH in the case of an acquisition by CCM, assuming a price of €750 million, financed with 30% debt and following the assumptions made above. Note that the accounting profitability for CCM's shareholders will be 8.9%,[2] while the economic profitability is 12.5%.

---

[2] Defined as ROE = net earnings/equity.

Table 3.7 Expected evolution of financial statements

New TCH operated by CCM						
Acquisition price: €15 per user						

Expected BS						
Years	Initial	1	2	3	4	5
Net Current Assets (NCA)	10.0	11.8	6.9	8.0	9.3	12.0
NFA (including goodwill)	740.0	757.8	779.7	806.9	840.4	883.6
Total net assets	750.0	769.6	786.6	814.9	849.7	895.6
Debt	243.4	262.0	274.3	287.1	298.4	307.4
Equity	506.6	507.6	512.3	527.8	551.3	588.3
Debt and equity	750.0	769.6	786.6	814.9	849.7	895.6

Expected profit and loss						
Years	Initial	1	2	3	4	5
Revenue		118.5	146.4	181.0	223.7	288.0
Cost of sales		−47.4	−58.6	−72.4	−89.5	−115.2
Gross margin		71.1	87.8	108.6	134.2	172.8
Operational expenses		−35.5	−19.3	−21.5	−24.8	−31.1
EBITDA		35.5	68.5	87.0	109.4	141.7
DA		−5.9	−7.3	−9.0	−11.2	−14.4
EBIT		29.6	61.2	78.0	98.2	127.3
Financial expenses		−12.2	−13.1	−13.7	−14.4	−14.9
EBT		17.4	48.1	64.3	83.8	112.4
Taxes		−4.4	−12.0	−16.1	−21.0	−28.1
Net earnings		13.1	36.1	48.2	62.9	84.3
To shareholders		−12.1	−31.3	−32.8	−39.3	−47.4
Retained earnings		1.0	4.8	15.4	23.5	36.9
Initial equity		506.6	507.6	512.3	527.8	551.3
Retained earnings		1.0	4.8	15.4	23.5	36.9
Final equity		507.6	512.3	527.8	551.3	588.3

Years	1	2	3	4	5	Average
return on investment	4.6%	8.7%	10.7%	12.9%	15.8%	10.5%
return on equity	2.6%	7.0%	9.1%	11.4%	14.3%	8.9%

Some Points to Negotiate

Assuming CCM is able to negotiate the initial offered price (€15 per user for the EV of TCH), it's clear how convenient it is to make an analysis like this, as it allows an understanding of the intrinsic assumptions that relate to our extrinsic valuation. As everybody knows, in any negotiation process it is crucial for negotiators to be prepared to discuss new proposals referring to any relevant issues, including the "small" detail of the price.

Table 3.8 Evaluation of TCH

Possible acquisition by CCM
Sensitivity analysis

	Base scenario	Price red 10% scenario 1	User red 10% scenario 2	Both 10% scenario 3
Users are differential	100.00%	100.00%	90.00%	90.00%
Initial price (Euros per user)	15.0	13.5	15.0	13.5
Economic profitability for CCM shareholders	12.50%	16.5%	8.90%	12.60%

Of course, this analysis can be complemented with a sensitivity analysis, deterministic and/or probabilistic, about the impact on economic profitability for CCM's shareholders brought about by changes in key value drivers: initial price, relevant users, expenses control, new capital structure and TV, to mention just a few. Table 3.8 summarizes some examples of sensitivity analysis.

According to this sensitivity analysis, a reduction of 10% in the initial price (to €13.5 per user) will increase the economic profitability of CCM shareholders to 16.5%. A similar reduction of 10% in the number of initial differential users will reduce this profitability to 8.90%, below the minimum expected profitability of 9.8%. A combined reduction of 10% in both the initial price and the initial differential users will have practically no effect on economic profitability.

Since the initial differential number of users is a relevant factor in determining the profitability of this operation, we can estimate the maximum reduction that CCM can afford while still generating the minimum expected profitability for its shareholders. A reduction of 7.6% will generate an economic profitability of 9.8%, with the present price. If CCM is able to renegotiate the price to €13.5 per user, the maximum reduction in users it can afford would be 17%.

A similar sensitivity analysis can be made with a more detailed expected evolution of revenue, in a similar way to the analysis developed in Table 3.3.

For example, if we assume that expected future revenue can be different because the buyer will be able to change the composition of its sources of revenue, selling more through more profitable channels, then the estimated EV of THC will increase significantly.

In Table 3.9 we can see a detailed explanation of the new EV of THC, assuming the following changes:

1. Different mix of revenues, selling more and spending less on advertising.
2. Reduction in cost of sales and operational expenses.
3. Same capital expenditure as in the previous scenario.

Table 3.9 Detailed forecast of revenue

Years	Now	1	2	3	4	5	
Users Detailed	50.0	55.0	60.0	65.0	70.0	75.0	in million
In volume							
Advertising	90.0%	85.0%	75.0%	65.0%	55.0%	50.0%	
Premium services	7.0%	7.0%	10.0%	10.0%	10.0%	10.0%	
Data sold	3.0%	8.0%	15.0%	25.0%	35.0%	40.0%	
	100.0%	100.0%	100.0%	100.0%	100.0%	100.0%	
In pricing							
Advertising	1.82	1.88	1.93	1.99	2.20	2.28	$ per user
Premium services	3.00	3.09	3.58	3.60	3.71	3.80	$ per user
Data sold	5.00	5.75	6.21	6.21	6.43	6.62	$ per user
Contribution to revenue							
Advertising	82.0	87.7	87.0	84.1	84.7	85.5	in million
Premium services	10.5	11.9	21.5	23.4	26.0	28.5	in million
Data sold	7.5	25.3	55.9	100.9	157.4	198.5	in million
Total revenue	100.0	124.9	164.4	208.4	268.1	312.5	in million
Initial Total Revenue	100.0	118.5	146.4	181.0	223.7	288.0	in million

Years	Now	1	2	3	4	5	
Total revenue	100.0	124.9	164.4	208.4	268.1	312.5	
Cost of sales		-50.0	-62.5	-75.0	-91.1	-100.0	From 40 to 32%
Gross margin		75.0	101.9	133.4	176.9	212.5	
Operational expenses		-37.5	-38.1	-43.4	-49.2	-57.6	From 30 to 20%
EBITDA		37.5	63.8	90.0	127.7	154.9	

DA		-6.2	-8.2	-10.4	-13.4	-15.6
EBIT		31.2	55.6	79.5	114.3	139.3
Taxes on EBIT (25%)		-7.8	-13.9	-19.9	-28.6	-34.8
EBIaT		23.4	41.7	59.7	85.7	104.5
FCF from operations		29.7	49.9	70.1	99.1	120.1
Evolution of Net Current Assets (NCA)						
Days of revenue	36.0	36.0	17.0	16.0	15.0	15.0
Net Current Assets (NCA)	10.0	12.5	7.8	9.3	11.2	13.0
FCF OWC		-2.5	4.7	-1.5	-1.9	-1.9
capital expenditure						
Maintenance		-6.2	-8.2	-10.4	-13.4	-15.6
New investments		-17.8	-22.0	-27.1	-33.5	-43.2
FCF capital expenditure		-24.0	-30.2	-37.6	-47.0	-58.8
Total FCF		3.2	24.5	31.0	50.3	59.4
TV						1,224.3
FCF to discount		3.2	24.5	31.0	50.3	1,283.7
EV	959.2					

Instead of number of users, can be based on the mix

This strategy using a different sales mix will improve the EV from €811.3 million to €959.2 million.

The Right Price in Mergers and Acquisitions (M&A)

After some years of decline owing to the financial crisis, in 2015 M&A activity is coming back to life, among other reasons because corporations and private equity funds are sitting on record amounts of cash and retained earnings, and they need to make that money work, especially in an environment of low interest rates. For example, in the USA M&A activity in 2015 finally reached pre-crisis levels.

According to a survey published by KPMG,[3] respondents expect to be more active in 2015 than in 2014: in 2014 almost 80% said their companies or funds made at least one acquisition, while in 2015 82% expect to make at least one acquisition. With 73% of the operations, the USA was the most attractive region for M&A investors, most probably because of its relatively healthy economy and receptive credit markets. Survey respondents were also attracted to Western Europe (14%) and China (12%). Not surprisingly, sectors expected to have the most deal activity were those characterized by transformation, including telecommunications, media and technology(TMT), with 62% of the answers.

The reasons a firm may want to acquire another are many and varied. Some aim to increase their market share or eliminate a troublesome competitor, while others seek the supposedly limitless advantages that the buyer can implement once it has acquired the target firm. The economic logic is very simple: company X wants to buy company Y because X believes that by managing Y it can give the resulting combination of X and Y greater value than the current total value of both firms.

We all know that the real world is full of surefire synergies that never happen, either because the acquiring firm overestimated the positive effects or because it underestimated the problems that always form part and parcel of the implementation of change in any organization. Numerous studies have shown that overpayment is one of the key factors in the failure of this kind of operation, and that paying over the odds is either down to a failure to rigorously assess the target's intrinsic value or to unrealistic expectations of synergies.

So how do you calculate the right price for an acquisition? Which key factors determine the price? What pitfalls must be avoided? How does the financing of the transaction affect the final price?

As in any negotiation process, a good price for an M&A transaction is the result of reaching a reasonable agreement on the EV of the company being

---

[3] KPMG 2015 M&A Outlook Survey.

acquired. For the price to be reasonable, the EV on which it is based must be likewise.

There is a Chinese proverb that says wisdom begins by calling things by their names. When we speak of EV we need to define what we mean. As already mentioned, there are essentially two types of EV: extrinsic or relative value; and intrinsic or fundamental value.

The relative value is based on external references. For example, the market value of a company is the value it is given during an M&A process, regardless of whether it takes place in a regulated market (a listed company) or in a private market (against comparable businesses). Other examples of extrinsic value include the liquidation value, the replacement value and the legal value. Insofar as the market is considered a reliable mechanism for allocating prices, an asset's extrinsic value is an appropriate reflection of its EV.

Of course, the market does not always work in this way. For this reason the intrinsic value, based on the more telling characteristics of the business, can provide a more solid measurement of EV. If the potential purchaser is interested in accounting metrics, he can use the adjusted book value, employing market or replacement value for adjustments. If, however, the potential buyer considers that the asset value provided by the books does not reflect the true EV of the business, then expected future cash flows that the target company will generate must be estimated, discounting them at a rate that correctly reflects the opportunity cost and the risks that are associated with them.

Contrary to common belief, relative (extrinsic) and fundamental (intrinsic) values are not incompatible; they are actually complementary. The difference between the two should serve to show the EV of control participation in the company.

Price and Relative Value

To establish a reasonable price using the relative value, it is important to make sure that the markets on which the comparison is based are comparable.

In the case of listed companies, not all capital markets have the same levels of efficiency, size and depth. Generally speaking, share prices provided by the financial markets in emerging and/or less developed countries do not usually reflect the true EV of the firms in question, and their use is therefore limited.

If the company is not listed and calculations are made on a like-for-like basis, it is important to make sure that the value reference used is consistent with the purpose of the valuation. For cross-border valuations it is not usually enough to use figures from transactions carried out by companies operating in the same sector or in a similar type of business. Consistency in terms of comparison can be analyzed using indicators that include the following:

1. Profitability, measured by the return on capital employed (ROCE).
2. The company's sustainable growth rate.
3. The company's size, measured by turnover.
4. The company's presence, measured by the level of diversification.

Other practices that ensure consistency in the terms of comparison include:

1. Use of recent figures.
2. Elimination of non-recurrent events.
3. Adjustment of value if non-operative results are produced.
4. Use of figures drawn up using comparable accounting principles.

Moreover, earnings per share (EPS) are often employed in valuations using comparable figures. Again, it is a good idea to ensure the consistency of these figures, especially when they are taken from companies involved in high-volume asset sales and purchases. In these cases, it is important to distinguish the earnings derived from ordinary or recurrent transactions from those that are the result of a non-recurrent transaction. For example, when General Electric (GE) announced the sale of its Japanese insurance subsidiary, GE Edison Life, in mid-2003, the company did not report the atypical earnings associated with the sale, which brought more than $2,000 million in revenue. Analysts estimated possible after-tax earnings at $250 million, which represented approximately $0.025 per share. Bearing in mind that the consensus figure on GE's EPS was $0.42, the impact of these atypical earnings was 6%.

Price and Fundamental Value

To obtain a reasonable price using the intrinsic value, it is essential to understand the valuation model used, the business being valued and how they adapt to each other. Accordingly, determining what a differential cash flow and an appropriate discount rate are and how they size up against each other depends on the position from where the valuation is being made. For example, if we were to try to determine the intrinsic value of a company, which we shall call A, in an acquisition by another company, which we shall call B, A's value will depend on the *why, for whom and the circumstances* of the valuation, which can bring about significant changes in the price. Table 3.10 shows some of the possible solutions that could serve in this case.

Take the case of the Spanish fast-food company Telepizza. In February 2006, the Ballvé brothers, who controlled the company with a 20.5% holding, announced a tender to purchase 100% of the capital at a price of €2.15 per share, which represented a premium of 14.36% on the share price at the last market close. When Telepizza's board of directors recommended that shareholders accept the offer, their advice was considered reasonable by all concerned. On May 5, however, the Portuguese group Ibersol announced an offer to buy 100% in cash and at €2.41 per share, which led to a

Table 3.10 Valuation

Possible Valuation Scenarios for A	
Scenario 1: Maximum value of A for B	
Differential cash flows:	Those generated by A when run by B
Synergies in A:	Included
Synergies in B:	Included
Discount rate:	A´s rate when run by B
What is obtained:	The maximum intrinsic value of A for B
What it is used for:	To determine, for B, the maximum price to be paid for A
Scenario 2: A's continuity value	
Differential cash flows:	Those generated by A without the transaction
Synergies in A:	Not included
Synergies in B:	Not included
Discount rate:	A's rate without the transaction
What is obtained:	A's intrinsic continuity value
What it is used for:	To determine A's minimum sale price
Scenario 3: B's continuity value	
Differential cash flows:	Those generated by B without the transaction
Synergies in A:	Not included
Synergies in B:	Not included
Discount rate:	B's rate without the transaction
What is obtained:	B's intrinsic continuity value
What it is used for:	To determine the possible A and B share exchange ratio, where applicable

modification of the initial offer made by the current owners, raising Telepizza's share price to €3.21 per share. This series of events raises several questions, including what had changed in the company between February and June for its value, in its current owners' opinion, to increase by almost 50%, and to what extent the recommendation of the company's board of directors created value for shareholders.

Indeed, price is a determining factor in the distribution of value that an M&A transaction can bring about. Let's remember the financial crisis that ensued when the Internet bubble burst with the subsequent effect on TMT companies between the first half of 2000 and the end of 2003. For example, a total of €110,000 million was paid for the 59 third-generation Universal Mobile Telecommunications System (UMTS) licenses for mobile phones awarded in European Union countries during the first few years of this century. And we should also mention the real estate overvaluation which led to the financial crisis that started in 2007.

In order to obtain the correct ratio between price and value it is essential to consider what is being bought and how it is being bought. For example, it is not the same to buy a controlling interest in a public company as it is to buy a non-controlling interest in a private company. Similarly, cash tenders are more attractive than tenders based on shares. Money makes it possible to buy new securities, and at times it is better to sell shares on the market than to accept a tender to purchase. Furthermore, there is always the risk that the transaction will not take place, and if the share value has increased considerably thanks to the potential transaction, investors can consider selling their securities and pocketing the cash. This alternative is particularly attractive when there are obstacles to the tender (from legal regulations, competitors, politics, etc.) or when there is a possibility of the transaction being delayed, a situation lately being encountered by a number of companies (Arcelor, Endesa, Metrovacesa, HP, etc.).

Once the value of the company has been made based on an open scenario, the process should be completed by examining real factors, such as possible limitations to the distribution of cash flows among those supplying the funds (capital and liabilities). These adjustments are particularly important when valuing M&A transactions in a multinational context, and must include an analysis of possible fiscal differences resulting from different rates of taxation between the two countries, the financing of the foreign company by the parent company once it has been acquired, and the alternatives available for repatriation of monetary flows to investors through various dividend share-out mechanisms.

Valuation Pitfalls

The importance of finding a reasonable price in M&A processes is evident. But it is also important not to fall into the traps that invariably appear when analyzing the price for this type of transaction.

Let's take a brief look at some common pitfalls:

Pitfall 1. Valuation should be left entirely to valuation experts.

A valuation process does, of course, require help from experts. But it also involves much more. All those involved in this process must understand the model being used, the assumptions on which it is based and its limitations and expectations, regardless of the fact that technical aspects may be outsourced to experts.

Pitfall 2. Failure to analyze the quality of the information.

In his last official meeting as President of the Securities and Exchange Commission in Philadelphia on January 16, 2001, Arthur Levitt pointed out that "A chat room is nothing but graffiti. If you are dumb enough to invest in what you see on a bathroom wall, you deserve what you get." Most probably this is not something most managers would do, but this reflection by someone who was also President of the American Stock Exchange might help us consider the importance of understanding information as a basis for valuation processes.

Pitfall 3. Failure to understand the context of the valuation.

A valuation process also involves a *why, for whom* and *in what circumstances* that have a marked effect on the final result. The answers to each of these questions must be clearly established. The subjective component of any economic valuation can only be based on these answers.

Pitfall 4. Failure to provide the right follow-up processes.

In 1994, BMW bought the British company Rover for approximately £8 million. Between 1995 and the end of 1999, it invested a further £2,000 million in Rover. During this time, Rover's share of the British car market fell from 13% to 5%. In May 2000, it was sold for less than £60 million. At the time, BMW's president, Joachim Milberg, commented: "We have learned that mergers can be paralyzing in certain circumstances."

In short, all valuations and the resulting price must be contrasted with the results. Insofar as a valuation is an opinion about the future, the basis for an acid test about how real this opinion actually is lies in the capacity for putting the chosen scenario into practice. This is why financial markets penalize the non-fulfillment of expectations very heavily indeed, and why companies need to handle all external and internal communications correctly. EV is based on the fulfillment of expectations, which in turn translates into credibility.

Analyzing the Case of Facebook and WhatsApp

In February 2014, Facebook (FB) announced the acquisition of WhatsApp (WHP) at a price of $19,000 million for the equity. Since WHP had around $60 million in debt, the transaction was made at an EV of $19,060 million.

From the very beginning, this operation was highly controversial not because of the opportunity taken for the takeover, but because of the price paid by FB. How can we have a better understanding of the economic consequences of paying $19,060 for WhatsApp?

Let's apply the methodology previously discussed in this book.

Understanding the Relative Value of WhatsApp

In relative terms, FB paid for WHP:

$$EV/users = 19,060/450 = \$42.4 \text{ per user}$$
$$EV/revenue = 19,060/ 400 = 47.7 \text{ times}$$

How do these figures fit with the market at that time?

In terms of money per user, FB was evaluated at €133 per user and Twitter at $117. Looking at the ratio to revenue, FB had a market capitalization of 22 times and Twitter one of 16 times. This gives us one of the key points towards understanding the price paid in relative terms: It only would make sense if FB was paying less per user, but with the hope to monetize them in terms of revenue and to generate future new FCFs.

Of course, to make this goal credible we should have specific information about what changes FB would introduce into the business model of WHP to make this happen, since at that time WHP was not generating positive FCFs.

Understanding the Intrinsic Value of WhatsApp

FB paid $19,060 million for WHP because it was believed that the EV of WHP was higher than that amount. Otherwise, all the eventual EV generated in this transaction would be captured by the sellers (shareholders of WHP before the operation).

This is a crucial point in understanding the economic consequences of the price associated with any M&A. Common sense tells us that the final agreed price should never be the maximum estimated value of the traded company, but somewhere in between the maximum and the minimum value.

Keeping this in mind, let's assume that the estimated value of the new WHP's EV, including all the synergies with FB, was $25,000 million. In this case, WHP would be paying $19,060 million for something with an estimated value of $25,000 million.

How can we justify this estimated EV?

Following the methodology developed in this chapter, we can estimate the level of TV associated with a reasonable evolution of the differential FCFs generated by WHP as a consequence of this acquisition. Once more, remember that these FCFs must be differential and sustainable, coming from new users or new business that FB will have only because of the acquisition of WHP.

Table 3.11 shows a proposal for this intrinsic evaluation of WHP, with a WACC of 8%.

Based on figures summarized in Table 3.11, we can note:

1. Apart from hidden agendas, we have to understand the changes FB will implement in the business model of the new WHP to generate these expected FCFs for Years 1 to 5.
2. Since this is a clear acquisition based on new markets and expansion, not on reduction of costs and expenses, synergies will come from new revenue.

Table 3.11 Estimated FCFs of WHP

Years	Today	1	2	3	4	5
FCF	−25,000	500	600	800	900	1,000
TV						32,392
Total		500	600	800	900	33,392
EV	25,000					

Figures in millions of US $

3. It's also crucial to analyze the expected differential revenue which will generate the FCFs required.

Naturally, this revenue will depend on the assumptions we make about the future operational policies FB will implement for WHP.

Assuming that EV will come from growth, we can estimate the evolution of the revenue in a situation where:

1. Operational variable costs and expenses will remain at 70% of revenue.
2. Operational fixed costs and expenses will be $200 million.
3. DA expenses will be 3% of revenue.
4. Tax rate will be 10%.
5. No investment needed in OWC.
6. Investment in capital expenditure will be equal to expenses in DA.

Table 3.12 summarizes this estimated evolution of revenue associated with the expected FCFs. Note that in Year 1 there are no taxes because of the tax shield coming from accumulated losses. We have also assumed that "available" revenue of the 450 million users of WHP would be the initial $400 million, if FB were able to make real the $1 per year and user...

The conclusion on this point is very clear: to generate the expected FCFs associated with this valuation, WHP would need an accumulated average annual growth rate in differential revenue of 123.4%. Not an easy task.

Additionally, the estimated EV in Year 5 has to be $32,392 million, which in terms of a perpetuity of the last FCF means a growth rate of around 4.7% forever – which becomes a growth rate of around 5.46% if we take as a base FCF an average of the five years. Again, not an easy task.

Understanding the Financing of this Operation

From the analysis of the price paid in this operation we can conclude that FB was placing a risky bet by paying $19,060 million for WHP, in the sense that there are reasonable doubts about how FB will monetize the users it got with WHP, not only in terms of needed growth, but also with regard to the right timing.

Unfortunately, when considering how this price was financed, our reasonable doubts about value creation grow.

Let's remember that these $19,000 million for the equity were financed without debt. FB used $7,000 million of cash in excess, and it issued 183 million new shares at the market price of $65.58.

Table 3.12 Expected evolution of FCF

Years		1	2	3	4	5
Revenue	400	2,593	3,210	4,032	4,445	4,855
Variable Costs and Expenses	-280	-1,815	-2,247	-2,822	-3,112	-3,399
Contribution Margin	120	778	963	1,210	1,334	1,457
Fixed Costs and Expenses	-100	-200	-200	-200	-200	-200
EBITDA	20	578	763	1,010	1,134	1,257
DA	-20	-78	-96	-121	-133	-146
EBIT	0	500	667	889	1,000	1,111
Taxes	0	0	-67	-89	-100	-111
EBIaT	0	500	600	800	900	1,000
DA	20	78	96	121	133	146
FCF from operations	20	578	696	921	1,033	1,145
FCF from OWC	0	0	0	0	0	0
Capital expenditure	-20	-78	-96	-121	-133	-146
FCF	0	500	600	800	900	1,000
Variation in revenue		548.3%	23.8%	25.6%	10.2%	9.2%

Figures in millions of US $

Table 3.13 Evolution of capital structure

Years		1	2	3	4	5
Equity	24,940	26,500	28,020	29,462	30,918	32,392
Debt	60	0	0	0	0	0
Valuation	25,000	26,500	28,020	29,462	30,918	32,392
Ke,l	8%	8%	8%	8%	8%	8%
WACC	8%	8%	8%	8%	8%	8%
FCF		500	600	800	900	1,000
ECF		500	600	800	900	1,000
TV						32,392
Total ECF	−19,000	500	600	800	900	33,392
IRR	14.4%					
If 1 share of FB is equal to 1 share of WHP						
New FB						
Old # shares 2,647	m					
New # shares 183						
Total shares 2,830						
% old shareholders	94%					
% of new shareholders	6%					

By doing this,

1. FB financed the operation without debt, renouncing the eventual EV creation derived from using the cheaper financial resource.
2. FB agreed on an exchange rate of 1 share of FB = 1 share of WHP.

These are quite debatable actions in terms of EV creation, especially for the old FB's shareholders.

In fact, if FB decides to maintain a capital structure in WHP without debt, the associated economic profitability of this acquisition for the shareholders of FB would be 14.4%. At an exchange rate of 1 share of FB = 1 share of WHP, the new shareholders would have 6% of the new FB. Of course, if the exchange rate had been different, this participation would also have changed (see Table 3.13).

What About an Implicit Real Option?

There is a complementary approach to understanding whether or not it is reasonable to pay $19,000 million for the equity of WHP. We can consider that, by buying WHP, FB is buying an option to sell the company in five years, at an estimated price. In this case, we should analyze the value of this real option to understand whether the $19,000 million paid makes sense. Technically, we should analyze a reasonable value of a put option on the shares of WHP in five years. Under what circumstances and assumptions would it make sense to evaluate this as being worth $19,000 million?

To calculate this value we can use the Black Scholes formula, considering the value of buying a European put option, at five years, with the following characteristics:

1. Value of the underlying asset	$25,000 million.
2. Exercise price	$35,000 million.
3. Volatility of the underlying asset	50%.
4. Time	five years.
5. Risk free rate	4%.

Note that we are making similar assumptions about the present estimated EV of WHP ($25,000 million) and about the TV needed in five years, as noted above. Under these assumptions, the value of this option would be $11.729 million, which again indicates an overvaluation of WHP at $19,000 million. Following this approach, to pay $19,000 million for the equity of WHP would only make sense if FB expects a value of WHP of $46,680 million in five years, while all the other assumptions remain unchanged.

With the exercise price of $35,000 million, even with a volatility of 100% of the price of the share of WHP, the value of the option would be below the proposed $19,000 million (see Table 3.14 and Fig. 3.2), which reinforces the idea of overvaluation.

Table 3.14 Volatility of the underlying asset and expected value of the option

Volatility	Expected value
50%	11,729
10%	4,632
20%	6,675
30%	8,635
40%	10,338
50%	11,729
60%	12,801
70%	13,581
80%	14,114
90%	14,455
100%	14,655

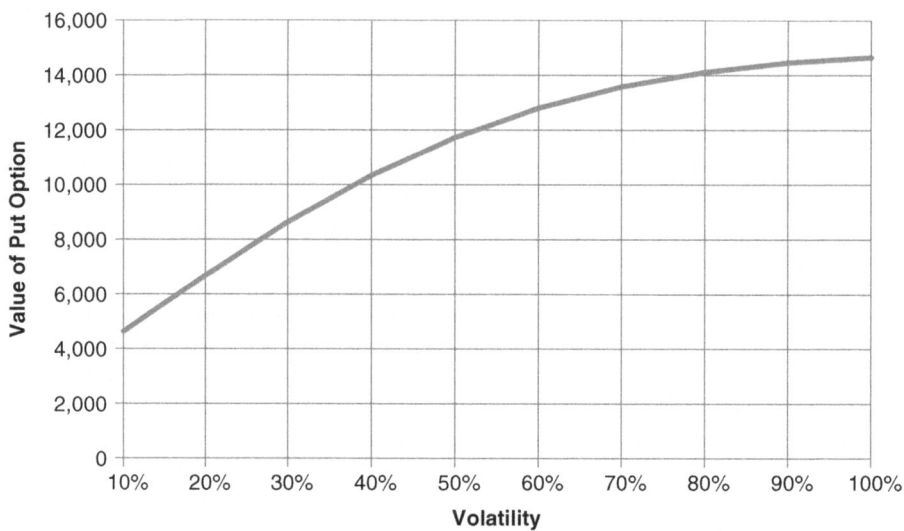

Fig. 3.2 Volatility of the underlying asset and expected value of the option

Some Conclusions About this Acquisition

Based on this analysis, we can summarize our conclusions about this operation:

1. This acquisition is based on future growth.
2. It makes sense from a strategic point of view.
3. The price of $19,000 million for the equity seems excessive.
4. This price will only be justified if FB is able to monetize the new users acquired with WHP.
5. One way to do this is to assume that:
   a. Differential revenue will grow at an accumulated average annual rate of 123.4% in the next five years.
   b. From that moment on, WHP will be able to grow at more than 5%, keeping its profitability forever, without new investments in OWC and in capital expenditure.
6. In any case, the acquisition was financed partially with new FB shares. In the accepted exchange rate between shares of FB and shares of WHP, there seems to be an excessive level of dilution for the old shareholders of FB.
7. Financed only with equity, the economic profitability for the shareholders is 14.4%. This would have been higher if the acquisition had also been financed with debt. For example, financed with a capital structure of 30%

Table 3.15 Expected capital structure with 30% of debt

Years		1	2	3	4	5
Equity	17,500	18,501	19,509	20,455	21,405	22,357
Debt	7,500	7,929	8,361	8,767	9,173	9,582
Valuation	25,000	26,430	27,870	29,222	30,578	31,939
Ke,u	8%	8%	8%	8%	8%	8%
Kd	6%	6%	6%	6%	6%	6%
Rf	4%	4%	4%	4%	4%	4%
MP	3%	3%	3%	3%	3%	3%
Be,u	1.30	1.30	1.30	1.30	1.30	1.30
Ke,l		8.7%	8.7%	8.7%	8.7%	8.7%
WACC	8.0%	7.7%	7.7%	7.7%	7.7%	7.7%
FCF		500	600	800	900	1,000
TV						31,939
FCF to be discounted		500	600	800	900	32,938
Discount factor		1.077	1.160	1.250	1.346	1.450
FCF at PV		464	517	640	669	22,710
EV	25,000					
FCF		500	600	800	900	1,000
Financ Exp (1-t)		−405	−428	−451	−473	−495
Amortization of principal		429	432	406	407	408
ECF		524	604	754	833	913
ECF		524	600	800	900	1,000
TV						22,357
Total ECF	−11,500	524	600	800	900	23,357
IRR	19.2%					

Ke,u = Cost of Equity Unleveraged

of debt, the economic profitability for the shareholders would have been 19.2% (see Table 3.15).

8. Complementarily, we can quantify this expected monetization of users by assuming that, with the acquisition of WHP, FB is buying a put option on the shares of WHP. According to some reasonable assumptions in line with the valuation made through DCF, the price of $19,000 million needs a final price for WHP above $46.6 billion.

What Happened Later?

At the end of 2015 there was a general consensus among financial analysts who recommended buying FB. From March 2014, the share price went from $73 to $105 (see Fig. 3.3), reflecting the important

2 Year

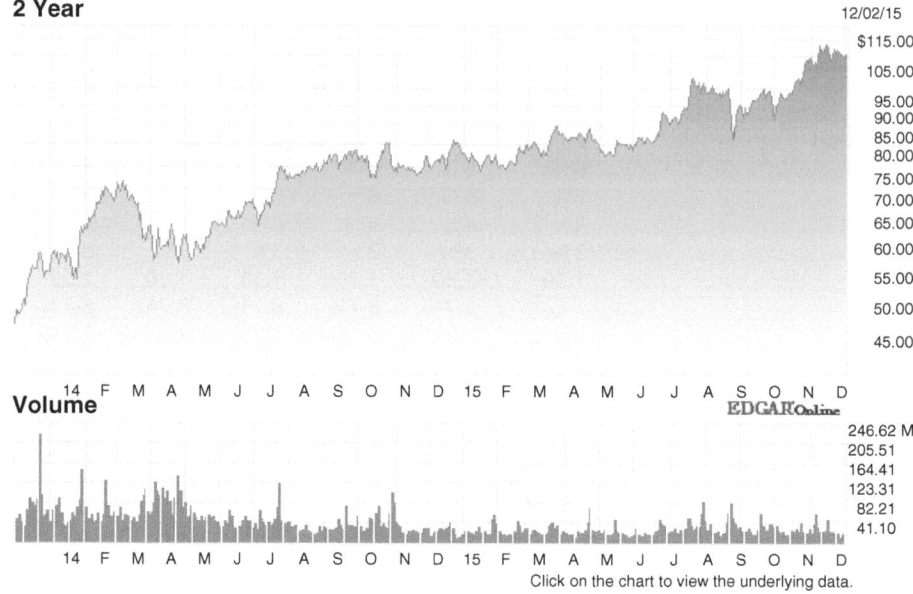

Fig. 3.3   Price share's evolution. Facebook

Source: Nasdaq

Table 3.16 Some data from Facebook

Fiscal year	2013	2014	2015
Total revenue	7,872	12,466	12,087
Net income	1,491	2,925	1.703
EPS	0.58	1.10	0.75

impact of WHP and other acquisitions in Facebook during 2014, as shown in Table 3.16.

Whether the momentum FB gathered in 2014 will remain is still not clear. In fact, during 2015 new WHP users grew by 250 million, and FB users by 200 million,[4] but this increase was not reflected in higher revenue. On the other hand, the net income of FB went down more than 50%, as a consequence, among other factors, of the natural increase in maintenance costs associated with new users.

Meanwhile, Facebook was keeping a huge amount in cash and equivalents (around $20,000 million).

---

[4] www.statista.com.

Evaluating Twitter

Let's consider now the case of Twitter, the company founded in 2006 as a provider of social networking and micro-blogging services through mobile devices and the Internet. In 2015 Twitter had more than 300 million users but also record losses that were not mitigated after its IPO in November 2013. The offer price was $26 per share, and since then the price has been highly volatile, as shown in Fig. 3.4.

The main question mark hanging over the future of Twitter is whether the company will be able to monetize the services provided to its users. So far, Twitter has been unable to do so, consistently showing losses and generating negative cash flow (see Table 3.17).

At the end of 2015 the market capitalization of Twitter was $17,500 million. Since the amount of debt was $1,602 million, the market value of Twitter was $19,102 million.

Does this valuation make sense?

In order to answer this question, one important point to consider is that Twitter is expected to generate a positive FCF in 2015. Based on this, we can

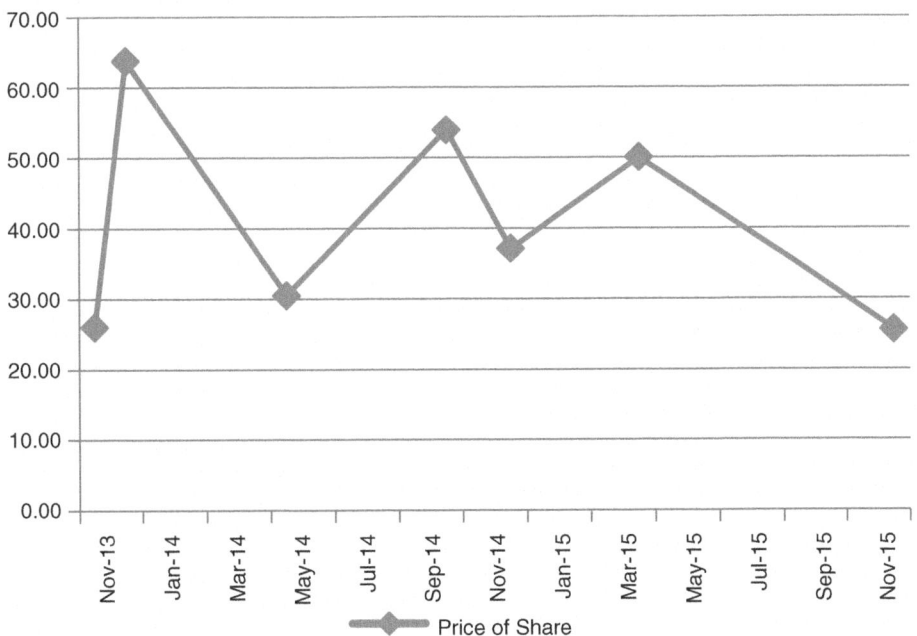

Fig. 3.4 Evolution of price of shares. Twitter

Table 3.17 Twitter: Evolution of profits

	2011	2012	2013	2014	2015
Profits	−67.3	−128.3	−79.4	−645.3	−577.8

Figures in million US$

Table 3.18 Expected evolution of future FCF

Years	1	2	3	4	5	6	7	8
FCF	91	121	161	214	285	379	504	33,136

Figures in millions of US$

estimate the future FCFs Twitter needs to generate to justify an EV of $19,102 million. These future FCFs can be estimated using an accumulative yearly growth rate (AYGR) and a TV. Table 3.18 summarizes a possible scenario to justify the market valuation of Twitter at the end of 2015.

These FCFs assume an AYGR of 33% and a TV of $30,556 million, equivalent to a ratio EV/EBITDA of 26.8.

Assuming a capital structure of 8% debt and 92% equity, the WACC is estimated at 8% and the EV is $19,102 million.

Once more: is it reasonable to assume that Twitter will be able to generate these future FCFs, including this TV?

Analyzing whether the Evaluation is Reasonable

Whether the FCF is Reasonable

One way to answer this is to analyze the numbers of users Twitter will need to generate these FCFs. Assuming that Twitter has 310 million users who generate a FCF of $91 million, the ratio FCF/users is 0.29 million. Based on this ratio, the expected evolution of number of users to generate the needed FCF will be (in millions):

Years	1	2	3	4	5	6	7	8
Needed FCF	91	121	161	214	285	379	504	670
#Needed users	310	412	548	729	970	1,290	1,716	2,282

Is it reasonable to assume this growth?

If we consider the historical growth of Twitter, in the last two years users increased at a rate of 14%. Assuming this rate of growth continues, we can estimate that the number of users and the ratio FCF/users that is required will reach the expected FCF, as follows:

Years	1	2	3	4	5	6	7	8
Expected # users	310	353	403	459	524	597	680	776
Needed FCF	91	121	161	214	285	379	504	670
Needed FCF/users	0.29	0.34	0.40	0.47	0.54	0.63	0.74	0.86

Again, is it reasonable to assume that Twitter will be able to increase the monetization of its users in order to reach the FCF/user ratio that is needed?

Additionally, we can analyze whether these FCFs are reasonable by using information based on the time spent daily per user on Twitter's website.

Considering that on average every user spends 20 minutes per day on Twitter's website, we can estimate that in the first year every user will contribute $12,470 per minute to the FCF in terms of time spent on the web page.

Based on these data, we can estimate the increase in minutes per day and per user that Twitter needs in order to generate the expected FCF (keeping constant the FCF/minutes spent):

Years	1	2	3	4	5	6	7	8	
Time spent daily	20	27	35	47	63	83	111	147	in minutes
Average daily FCF per minute spent	12.47	12.47	12.47	12.47	12.47	12.47	12.47	12.47	in 000 US$

The estimated increase in FCF per minute spent Twitter needs to generate the expected FCF (keeping constant the time spent):

Years	1	2	3	4	5	6	7	8	
Time spent daily	20	20	20	20	20	20	20	20	in minutes
Average daily FCF per minute spent	12.47	16.58	22.05	29.33	39.01	51.88	69.00	91.77	in 000 US$

In summary, to achieve the needed FCF, Twitter will need:

1. To increase the number of users from 310 million to 2,282 million in eight years, if the company maintains the current FCF/user ratio. This means an AYGR of 33%.
2. To increase the FCF/user ratio from $0.29 million to $0.86 million in eight years, if the company has an increase in users with an AYGR of 14%.

3. To increase the time spent daily per user on the website from 20 minutes to 147 minutes, if the company keeps constant the ratio of average daily FCF per minute spent.
4. To increase the average daily FCF per minute spent from $12,470 to $91,770, if the company keeps at a constant the time spent daily on the website by each user.

Whether the TV is Reasonable

Assuming Twitter will be able to generate the estimated FCFs included in the valuation, the required TV is $30,556 million.

In terms of EV/EBITDA, this TV implies a ratio of 26.8 times.

This TV is equivalent to the value of its last FCF growing at an annual rate of 5.68% and this continuing forever.

Both extrinsic and intrinsic comparisons lead to an overvalued TV.

Some Conclusions on Twitter's Valuation

1. The main question mark hanging over the future of Twitter is whether the company will be able to monetize the services provided to its users. So far, Twitter has been unable to do this, consistently showing losses and generating negative cash flow.
2. At the end of 2015 the market capitalization of Twitter was $17,500 million. Since the amount of debt was $1,602 million, the market value of Twitter was $19,102 million.
3. To analyze whether Twitter's EV is reasonable, we have to justify the required evolution of the expected FCFs and TV.
4. In terms of FCF, Twitter will need:
   a. To increase the number of users from 310 million to 2,282 million in eight years, if the company maintains the current FCF/user ratio. This means an AYGR of 33%.
   b. To increase the FCF/user ratio from $0.29 million to $0.86 million in eight years, if the company sees an increase in the number of users with an AYGR of 14%.
   c. To increase the time each user spends daily on the website from 20 minutes to 147 minutes, if the company keeps constant the ratio of average daily FCF per minute spent.
   d. To increase the average daily FCF per minute spent from $12,470 to $91,770, if the company maintains the time spent daily per user at a constant level.

5. In terms of TV, Twitter must have a final value of 26.8 times its last EBITDA. And it is equivalent to the value of its last FCF growing at an annual rate of 5.68% and forever.

Summary

1. When we evaluate a company we want to have a reasonable answer to the question of how much we would pay for that company, considering its EV. This means that any valuation is an opinion and, like any opinion, it can be a very reasonable judgment or complete nonsense.
2. To get a reasonable valuation we need to focus it. To focus any valuation we have to clarify issues such as what we want to evaluate; for what purpose we want to evaluate a company; from what perspective we want to evaluate a company; under what circumstances we want to evaluate a company.
3. Contrary to common belief, relative (extrinsic) and fundamental (intrinsic) values are not incompatible and are actually complementary. The difference between the two should serve to show the EV of a control participation in the company.
4. To establish a reasonable price using the relative value it is important to make sure that the markets on which the comparison is based are comparable.
5. To obtain a reasonable price using the intrinsic value it is essential to understand the valuation model used, the business being valued and how they adapt to each other.
6. In order to obtain the correct ratio between price and value it is essential to consider what is being bought and how it is being bought. For example, it is not the same to buy a controlling interest in a public company as it is to buy a non-controlling interest in a private company.
7. Once the value of the company has been made based on an open scenario, the process should be rounded off by examining real factors, such as possible limitations to the distribution of cash flows among those supplying the funds (capital and liabilities).
8. These adjustments are particularly important when valuing M&A transactions in a multinational context, and must include an analysis of possible fiscal differences resulting from different rates of taxation between two countries, the financing of the foreign company by the parent company once it has been acquired and the alternatives available

for repatriation of monetary flows to investors through various dividend share-out mechanisms.

9. These valuation principles can be applied to any business transaction in order to understand the impact of key value drivers on the final price and whether the assumptions used to reach that price are reasonable.

In transactions dealing with the digital world, it is common to justify prices based on the number of users. By applying these concepts about EV we can better understand the implicit assumptions needed to make possible the monetization of these new users.

4

Weighing the Air: Valuing Digital Intangibles

Introduction

In this chapter we will continue to analyze some business transactions which have taken place in the digital economy in recent years, in order to discuss whether the prices paid were reasonable.

Instagram's Acquisition by Facebook

In April 2012, Facebook (FB) announced the acquisition of Instagram (IG), the popular photo-sharing application, at a price of $1,000 million in cash and stock.

At that time IG had 30 million users and was one of the most downloaded applications on the iPhone. One week earlier, IG released a version of its application for Google's Android operating system.

In terms of enterprise value/users, Facebook paid $33 per user for Instagram, with the idea of monetizing these new users. One year later, Instagram had 150 million users, but was still not generating direct revenue.

Does this mean that the price paid by FB was excessive? Why did FB buy IG? How can we justify the price paid?

© The Author(s) 2017
F. López Lubián, J. Esteves,, *Value in a Digital World*,
DOI 10.1007/978-3-319-51750-6_4

Understanding the Intrinsic Value of Instagram

Applying the same methodology as that used to analyze the acquisition of WhatsApp (WHP) in Chapter 3, we can assume that if FB paid $1,000 million for IG it is because FB believed that the enterprise value (EV) of IG was higher. Let's assume that a reasonable EV for the IG owned by FB was $1,500 million. Can we justify this estimated EV of $1,500 million?

In terms of differential and sustainable free cash flow (FCF) coming from this operation, we can estimate the FCF required for the first year to have a present value (PV) of $1,500 million, providing a time horizon of five years, an annual accumulative growth of 4% in the FCF, a terminal value (TV) equal to the value of a perpetuation of the FCF of the previous year, growing ad infinitum at 3%, and a weighted average cost of capital (WACC) of 10%.

As detailed in Table 4.1, the initial FCF would be $213.4 million.

Do these numbers make sense? Can they be considered reasonable as a measure of realistic synergies associated with this operation?

Unfortunately, there is no information available on the differential contribution of FCF to FB coming from the acquisition of IG. However, we can summarize the reasons why FB bought IG, and consider the possibilities of differential FCF generated by that operation.

It is commonly agreed that FB bought IG because:

1. FB would gain access to images and young users not available without IG.
2. IG's acquisition by FB would give IG muscles to grow without new investments in needed infrastructure.
3. FB would increase its revenue derived from mobile ads, generating new profits.

Table 4.1 Estimated differential FCF coming from IG

Years		1	2	3	4	5
FCF		−1,500.0	213.4	221.9	230.8	240.0	249.6
TV (g = 3%)							3,672.5
FCF		−1,500.0	213.4	221.9	230.8	240.0	3,922.1
WACC	10%						
EV	1,500.0						

Figures in millions of US $

To implement these expected synergies, in 2013 FB set up an app to make IG available to mobiles. From 2012 to 2015 the number of IG users grew from 30 million to more than 400 million. There are no doubts about the economies of scale that the existing FB's infrastructure produced in IG.

Have these expected synergies been reflected in FB's results?

On January 27, 2016, FB reported a quarter of soaring revenue. For 2015 the company reported $3,690 million profit on $17,930 million in revenue, an increase of 44% from 2014. The results were largely a result of FB's enormous success in selling advertising on mobile devices, a business that the company had not even been in just a few years earlier. In 2015 mobile ads made up 80% of FB's total ad business in the fourth quarter, compared to 23% in the same quarter of 2012.

Additionally, in 2015 FB had 1.59 billion visitors per month, up 14% from a year before. About 1.44 billion of those people visited the site on a mobile device.

As noted already, FB does not disclose the portion of revenue that IG accounts for in overall sales. On January 29, 2016 Sheryl Sandberg, chief operating officer of FB, said in an interview that 98 of the top advertisers on FC also advertised on IG in the last quarter of 2015.[1] At the end of 2015 IG had more than 400 million regular monthly users.

Table 4.2 summarizes some financial figures for FB in recent years.

Valuation as a Real Option

Now we can use a complementary approach to understand how reasonable (or not) it was to pay $1,000 million for the equity of IG. We can consider that, by buying IG, FB is buying an option to sell IG in five

Table 4.2 FB evolution of some figures

Years	2013	2014	2015
Revenue	7,872	12,466	17,928
Income from operations	2,804	4,994	6,225
Net income	1,490	2,925	3,669

---

[1] New York Times, January 29, 2016.

years, at an estimated price. In this case, we should analyze the value of this real option to understand whether that $1,000 million makes sense. Technically, we should analyze a reasonable value of a put option on IG's shares in five years. Under what circumstances and assumptions would it make sense to evaluate this option at $1,000 million?

To calculate this value we can use the Black Scholes formula, considering the value of buying a European put option at five years with the following characteristics:

• Value of the underlying asset	• $1,500 million
• exercise price	• $3,673 million
• Volatility of the underlying asset	• 50%
• Time	• five years
• Risk free rate	• 4%

Note that we are making similar assumptions about the present estimated EV of IG ($1,500 million) and the TV required in five years, as commented on above. Under these assumptions, the value of this option would be $1,740 million, which indicates no overvaluation of IG at $1,000 million. Following this approach, to pay $1,000 million for the equity of IG would only imply overvaluation if FB expects IG to have a value of $2,583 million in five years and all other assumptions remain unchanged.

With the exercise price of $3,673 million, even with a volatility of 10% in the price of IG's shares, the value of the option would be above $1,000 million (see Table 4.3 and Fig. 4.1), which reinforces the idea of there being no overvaluation.

Table 4.3 Volatility of the underlying asset and expected value of the option

Volatility	Expected value
50%	1,740
10%	1,507
20%	1,528
30%	1,592
40%	1,670
50%	1,740
60%	1,791
70%	1,823
80%	1,837
90%	1,838
100%	1,830

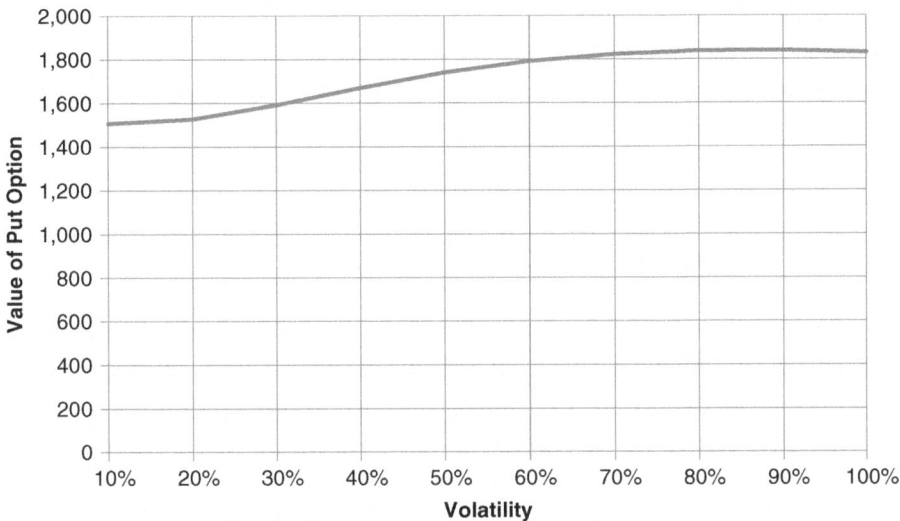

Fig. 4.1 Volatility of the underlying asset and expected value of the option

Some Conclusions About this Operation

Based on this analysis, we can summarize some conclusions:

1. FB's acquisition of IG was based on future growth.
2. It made a lot of sense from a strategic point of view.
3. The price of $1,000 million for the EV looked excessive at the time of the operation, mainly because IG was evaluated some months before at half that price.
4. In any case, this price will only be justified if FB is able to monetize the new users acquired with IG.
5. One way to do this is to assume that:
    a. Starting with an initial differential free cash flow (FCF) of $213.4 million, IG will need to generate additional FCF growing at an accumulated average annual rate of 4% in the next four years.
    b. TV at the end of Year 5 must be equal to the value of a perpetuation of the FCF of the previous year, growing forever at 3%, and with a WACC of 10%.
6. Although there is no information available on the differential contribution of FCF to FB arising from the acquisition of IG, the evolution of FB in 2013–2015 was very successful in terms of revenue, operational profit and net profit. One key factor to generate this success was

the development of ads sales to mobile devices, partially brought about by the acquisition of IG.

7. In comparison with the 2014 acquisition of WHP, analyzed in Chapter 3, this operation makes more sense both in terms of the price paid and of how reasonable the expected synergies are which can justify that price.

What's Going on With the Unicorns?

In recent years, the number of unicorns (private technology startups with a market valuation of more than $1,000 million) has increased dramatically. At the end of 2015 there were 144 unicorns valued at $505,000 million, about five times as many as three years before.

Since most of these unicorns are unprofitable and have not met their growth targets, it might seem difficult to understand why investors with a conservative profile, such as mutual funds, have been investing in these companies at these prices.

Some investors in unicorns bet that a new generation of technology companies will replace the old guard (Amazon, Google and FB), evaluating them as if they were guaranteed to be among the long-term winners and sole survivors in their line of business. This may be an explanation of the volatility in values and prices that these companies experienced during 2015.

But the other side of the coin is that many of these unicorns were agreeing to investors' demands to attach special privileges to the shares being sold. In fact, many major investors were asking for favorable terms such as liquidation preferences to participate in financing rounds. According to these agreements, investors are guaranteed some additional returns and/or get at least their money back. In other cases, investors were offered "ratchets," meaning they will receive additional shares to compensate for losses in valuation when the company goes public.

This was the case for Square, a mobile payment firm that went public in November 2015. From a valuation of $6,000 million in a previous fundraising round, the company went public with an offer price of $4,000 million. In that initial public offering (IPO), late-stage investors in Square were protected with ratchets.

The bottom line is clear: when you are evaluating a company (whether it is a unicorn or not) you should know exactly what you are valuing, especially if you're the buyer.

If you're investing in a company which is looking for finance in a down round, at lower valuations than previous levels, be sure that you understand the eventual conflict of interest between new money and old. Old money may sit back and rely on the anti-dilution rights and liquidation preferences to protect itself from the new money.

In cases like this, the new money (you) should evaluate the company (unicorn or not) considering possible issues that include the following:

1. Changes in the expected (FCF due to the loss of key employees.
2. How much of these expected FCF will really be free for the new shareholders?
3. Changes in the investment's risks, derived from operational and financial aspects.

Any down round is a "lemon" signal to the market, indicating that the company's business plan is not working properly. Since most unicorns compensate employees with shares, in down round situations it could be difficult for former unicorns to keep key employees after destroying the value of their shares. In late 2015, Jawbone undertook a down round at roughly half its previous $3,000 million financing, carving out additional common shares for employees to make up for their loss.

If stock options incentives do not work, then it may be necessary to set up cash bonus plans or other cash-based incentives plans to motivate success. The problem will be that it isn't as good as cold-hard stock that has potential for a big payout. If the labor market is flexible and has opportunities, chances are that good employees will move to the next start up and take their chances there.

But it is not only a matter of changes in the expected and reasonable FCF, but also in the possibility of obtaining them. If the evaluation goes below the liquidation preference, the common shareholders will have their entire investments wiped out. Consequently, if you are assuming a riskier position, you should ask for higher reward.

Consequently, lower than expected FCF, with a higher risk of not being totally free, should lead to a lower economic value of the company and a higher value for your investment.

An example will help to clarify these issues.

The IPO of Square

In November 2015, Square, the payment technology company founded and led by Twitter chief executive officer (CEO) Jack Dorsey, raised $243 million by pricing its IPO at $9 per share, which implied a market value of around $2.9 billion.

In previous months, Square had raised $180 million in private funding at $15.46 per share, in a multi-stage Series E round stretching from September 2014 to October 2015. Square's Series D round, which was raised in September 2012, valued the company at $11.01 per share.

At that time, the price of Square's IPO was considered a major disappointment for the San Francisco-based company, which had expected to price its 27 million shares at between $11 and $13 each.

As a consequence, holders of Series E stock received extra shares in the IPO, in order to help make up for the underwhelming pricing. These investors were protected by a ratchet. While they had bought shares at a price of $15.46, the company guaranteed them at least a 20% return on that investment. In order to make this happen when it priced its shares at $9 each, Square was required to issue an estimated 10.3 million shares – valued at nearly $93 million at the IPO price – to those investors. Those shares were worth a collective $135 million when the market closed, on December 2.

While investors with ratchets benefited from the provision, Square's employees did not. Because the company was obliged to issue more stock to those Series E investors, the entire share pool was diluted. At a Silicon Valley tech firm, where employees are often attracted to companies based on the type of equity packages they receive, this will not sit well with a mid-level engineer or designer who may have given up a cushy job at Google for Square and its equity. Come the expiration of the lockup period, which prevents investors and those inside the company from selling, employees may find themselves in a tougher market if they want to offload their shares.

What happened to the share price of Square is a typical example of volatility due to speculative reasons, an approach to value quite different from the one that comes from an investment approach. When the company was private, the price of the share reached a pick of $15.46, an overvaluation based on the fact that 88.5% of the new shares were protected by a ratchet. The remaining 11.5% holders of Series E stock were clearly overvalued at that price, because they didn't have any guarantee of a return on their investment.

Did it make sense to pay $15.46 per share for Square in 2015? Was this price/value sustainable?

Table 4.4 shows a summary of financial information over the last years for Square.

At the end of 2014 it was quite difficult to believe that paying $15.46 per share for Square was reasonable, unless you had some kind of agreement to guarantee a given level of profitability.

Table 4.4 Square. Some financial information

Evolution of some financial information Square			
	2012	2013	2014
Revenue	203,499	552,433	850,192
Gross profit	64,551	128,785	226,074
Operating result	−85,361	−104,942	−150,491
FCF from operations	−85,361	−104,942	−148,439

Thousands of US $

In Table 4.5 we analyze the TV of Square needed over six years in an evaluation of the company where:

1. FCF will become positive in Year 3.
2. The last FCF will be $100 million.
3. WACC is 10%.

This estimated TV of $3,804 million implies an evaluation of Square in Year 6 in which the permanent and accumulated growth rate is higher than 7%. This implicit growth of 7.18% looks neither reasonable nor sustainable.

Note that if we use this intrinsic value approach to analyze the price of $9.0 per share offered in the IPO, the estimated TV of Square needed becomes $2,601 million, which means a growth of 5.93%, which is still not reasonable (see Table 4.6).

Table 4.5 Valuation

Years		1	2	3	4	5	6
FCF		−74,220	0	25,000	50,000	75,000	100,000
TV							2,601,769
Total FCF		−74,220	0	25,000	50,000	75,000	2,701,769
EV	1,557,108						
D	30,000						
E	1,527,108						
# shares	169,679						
Price of share	9.00						
FCF	100,000						
g	5.93%						
WACC	10%						
TV	2,601,375						

Table 4.6 An estimated TV in the IPO

Years		1	2	3	4	5	6
FCF		−74,220	0	25,000	50,000	75,000	100,000
TV							2,601,769
Total FCF		−74,220	0	25,000	50,000	75,000	2,701,769
EV	1,557,108						
D	30,000						
E	1,527,108						
# shares	169,679						
Price of share	9.00						
FCF	100,000						
g	5.93%						
WACC	10%						
TV	2,601,375						

Figure 4.2 summarizes some information released in the IPO.

At the beginning of 2016, the evolution of Square's share price reflected this estimated overvaluation. From a peak of almost $15 per share in November, on February 1 the share closed at $8.76, a price very close to the 52-week low of $8.27.

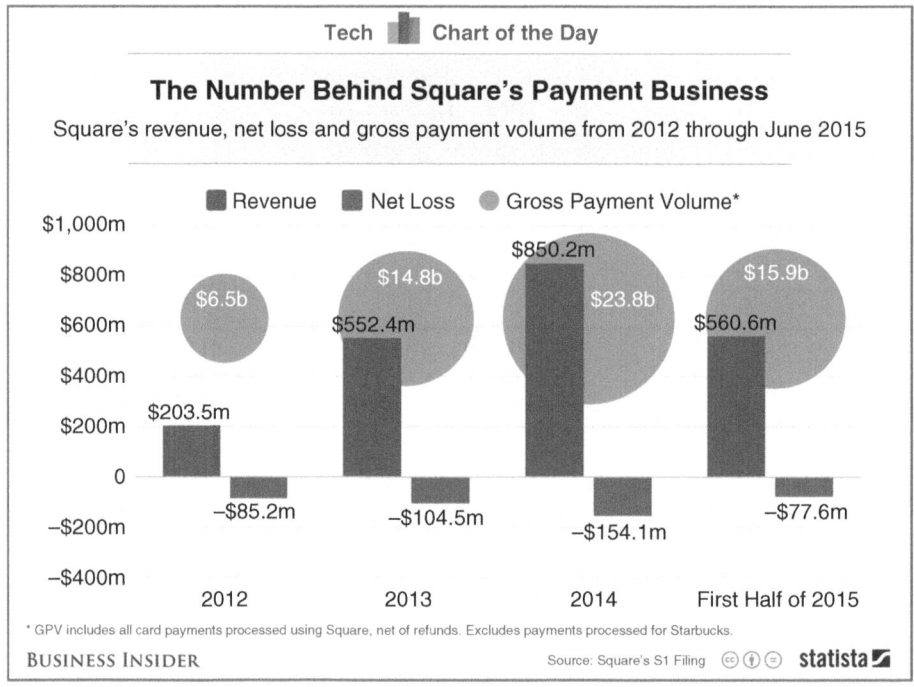

Fig. 4.2 The numbers behind Square's payment business

The Expected IPO of Ant Financial Services

In March 2016, Ant Financial Services Group announced that it was planning to raise up to 20 billion yuan ($3.1 billion) in a new funding round from a clutch of new and existing investors, with an estimated valuation of more than $50 billion. According to the company, this valuation would also set the stage for Ant Financial's future IPO, expected in 2017.

Ant Financial Services (AFS) has its origin in the transfer in 2011 of Alipay, China's most used online platform, from Alibaba Group. Renamed AFS in 2014, the company grew beyond just online payments to incorporate new services such as micro lending, banking and credit scores.

In 2016 AFS had more than 400 million active annual users, offering products and services linked to Alibaba, such as the online payment platform Alipay, Yu'e Bao, an online money market fund, and My Bank, an online bank.

Alipay controlled more than 82% of China's online payment market, according to data from iResearch. It processed around 120 million transactions per day, when the estimated number of all Chinese daily non-cash transactions was 170 million (including bills, bank cards and all electronic transfers).

How can we know whether or not this valuation of AFS was reasonable? Is this valuation just an attempt to increase the price for the coming IPO due in 2017?

If we look at a comparable situation, in 2014 Alibaba launched an IPO at a price which implied an EV of $25 billion, but at that time AFS was not included in Alibaba. In 2015 AFS raised $1.8 billion in a first round of fundraising, with a base value of $45 billion.

After just one year of operations, WeBank raised money in 2015 at a valuation of $5.5 billion. We Bank is a unit of Internet giant Tencent Holdings Ltd, which competes with AFS's My Bank.

Companies such as AFS can use their vast troves of data and analytics to reduce the risk of lending to small borrowers, a market with huge potential in China. Additionally, with Alipay and other products, AFS is able to keep a finger on the pulse of each and every customer: their shopping history, utility bills, work and home addresses, and so on. Armed with this information, AFS can establish accurate credit profiles of customers, based on which it can offer a variety of credit-related services.

According to Jing Xiandong, President of AFS, the company's goal is to build up a new and truly inclusive financial system on the Internet that better serves small business and the public.

Whether or not FSA will be able to achieve this goal determines the importance of the speculation component in AFS's $50 billion valuation.

Lessons from Unicorns' Valuations

Let's summarize some lessons we can learn from the analysis just undertaken.

1. For any extrinsic valuation, try to understand the influence of short-term (speculative) movements on the market value.
2. Decide the type of investor you want to be: short term and speculative; or long term and looking for sustainable value.
3. Estimate the sustainability of the market price based on a reasonable intrinsic valuation.
4. Select a key value driver (KVD) and determine the reasonability of the assumptions you need on this KVD in order to get the present market value.
5. Be aware of the type of share you are buying, in terms of liquidity, control and rights.

Some Findings from Research

A report published in 2016 by the consulting firm Play Bigger determined that companies that went public between their sixth and tenth years were more successful than those that went public earlier or later.[2] The study looked at startup firms' market capitalization. It also determined that companies that are leaders in their categories created most of their value after going public.

The researchers began by exploring speed. They took the market capitalizations of 1,125 firms that started in the year 2000 or later and divided each by the number of years since founding; the result was the "time to market cap." A company founded five years ago that is worth $2 billion, for example, has a greater time to market cap than a company founded ten years ago that is worth $3 billion. For firms that have gone public, the market cap is the total value of outstanding shares; for private firms, it is the valuation assigned by venture capitalists during the most recent round of funding (private valuations are less precise, but they are arguably the best approximation of value creation).

---

[2] "Time to Market Cap: The New Metric That Matters," by Al Ramadan, Christopher Lochhead, Dave Peterson and Kevin Maney.

The results were even more dramatic than the researchers expected. Firms founded from 2012 to 2015 had a time to market cap more than twice that of firms founded between 2000 and 2003. In other words, today's startups are growing about twice as fast as those founded a decade ago.

Additionally, these researches scored the companies in its sample on the basis of whether they were trying to create entirely new categories of products or services in order to fill needs that consumers did not realize they had. They looked at whether firms are articulating new problems that cannot be solved by existing solutions and whether they are cultivating large and active developer ecosystems, among other criteria. They found that the vast majority of post-IPO value creation comes from companies they call "category kings," which are carving out entirely new niches; think of FB, LinkedIn and Tableau. Those niches are largely "winner take all" – the category kings capture 76% of the market.

Tech start-ups are in a race to define new product categories, and the pace has quickened. Simply raising more money isn't enough to win this race, and going public too soon or too late may limit long-term success. Even for unicorns, the path forward can be a challenge.

Buying a Brand: The Case of Tuenti

In August 2010, Telefónica announced the purchase of 90% of Tuenti, a social network designed to become the Spanish alternative to FB. At that time Tuenti had an estimated 14 million users, mostly young people.

The final price for this 90% was €70 million, based on the valuation of Tuenti made in March 2010 for the last issue of new equity.

With this acquisition, Telefónica wanted to become a player in social networks, trying to monetize these young users by offering them a low-cost provider of mobile phones (Operador Móvil Virtual) and adding value through the offer of new services.

Additionally, this acquisition would provide Tuenti with the needed financial muscle to expand not only in Spain but also in Latin American countries. Expected new users would multiply the present number, and eventually they would become mobile phone customers.

In short, Telefónica was making a strategic move to be present in social networks, using the Tuenti brand to generate new users and to gain new customers in the mobile phone business, either through a new low cost provider (Tuenti Móvil, launched at the beginning of 2012) or through its existing mobile phone company (Movistar).

In November 2013, Telefónica bought the remaining 10% of Tuenti because the minority shareholders exercised their option to sell. The amount was not disclosed, but if we assume a similar price to the first acquisition the value of this 10% was €7.8 million.

Was this acquisition a logical and reasonable strategic movement for Telefónica? Did the price agreed make sense?

From the perspective of 2010, the answer to both questions is yes.

Apart from the reasons already noted, the acquisition of Tuenti by Telefónica was strategically relevant because in a context of financial crisis, low cost providers of mobile phone services, such as Pepephone or Yoigo, were eroding Telefónica's customers.

If we analyze the price using our intrinsic valuation model, we can estimate that, in 2010, a reasonable value for Tuenti, owned by Telefónica and implementing the expected synergies, was higher than €70 million for 90% of the company.

In Table 4.7 we summarize a possible valuation of the new Tuenti. Note that in this valuation we use quite conservative assumptions:

1. Operational FCF would increase from negative (first year) to zero (second year), reaching an amount of €15 million in the last year.
2. Tuenti would also need additional investment in marketing and fixed assets in order to reinforce its brand's recognition and image.
3. The WACC is 8.2%, as shown in Table 4.8. We are considering a conservative capital structure for Tuenti.
4. TV comes from a perpetuation of the FCF of the previous year, growing at 3%.

In summary, according to the information we had in 2010, Tuenti's acquisition from Telefónica at that price made a lot of sense, providing the buyer was able to implement the expected synergies in the purchased company.

Table 4.7 An estimated EV for Tuenti acquired by Telefónica

Years		1	2	3	4	5
Acquisition				−8		
Estimated operating FCF		−5	0	5	10	15
Estimated investment		−5	−5	−6	−7	−8
TV						139
Total FCF		−10	−5	−9	3	146
EV	80					

Table 4.8 Estimated WACC of Tuenti

Kd	5.0%
Ke	9.0%
E	80.0%
D	20.0%
t	0.0%
WACC	8.2%

What Went Wrong?

At the beginning of February 2016, Tuenti announced that the company would be gradually discontinuing its social network, trying to focus its activity on mobile phones. The company recognized that most of the users in its social network were migrating to other networks, such as FB or IG. It had lost millions of users from its social network, and they had not been offset by new customers in the mobile phone business, estimated at that time to be worth 0.27 million.

If we analyze Tuenti's evolution from 2010 to 2015, we can understand what happened with the expected synergies which motivated the acquisition.

The evolution of active users of the social network was the following:

2010 Estimated 14 million active users
2012 Estimated 10 million active users
2013 Estimated 6 million active users
2014 Estimated 4.2 million active users
2015 Estimated 1.5 million active users
2016 Social network discontinued

What happened? What went wrong?

This can be considered to be a typical example of a poorly implemented logical strategy. With the acquisition of Tuenti, Telefónica was buying access to the social network business through a recognized brand. One mistake was not to invest in the brand. A key element in Telefónica's strategy for Tuenti was to retain new mobile phone customers who were using a strong brand, which means a sustainable and growing number of active users. While Tuenti was losing active users, there was not an appropriate response from the company that would keep them, which would offer services they really wanted.

Table 4.9 Some financial information for Tuenti

Years	Sales	Results
2010	NA	−10.0
2011	10.5	−11.7
2012	17.1	−11.3
2013	16.9	−20.8
2014	21.1	−16.0

Figures in million Euros
Source: Tuenti

Tuenti became a weak brand because of its inappropriate reaction to the competition coming from other social networks (FB, IG) and from other low cost mobile phone companies (Pepephone).

According to former managers of Tuenti, its erratic and changing strategy produced an important exit of key people, who were used to a different company culture.

In Table 4.9 we summarize the evolution of Tuenti's key financial data from 2010 to 2014.

Based on this information, we can estimate the differential cash flows generated in Telefónica because of the purchase of Tuenti.

We estimate these figures by:

1. Assuming that results of Tuenti reasonably reflect the FCF generated.
2. Considering changes in Telefónica's stake in Tuenti.
3. Including the net movement of cash between the companies.

Table 4.10 includes these estimations.

Table 4.10 Estimated differential FCF for Telefónica

Years	Results = FCF	Telefónica Participation	Acquisition of Tuenti	Cash moved between comp.	Estimated Diff Cash flow
			−70.0		−70.0
2010	−10.0	0.9			−9.0
2011	−11.7	0.9			−10.5
2012	−11.3	0.9		5.5	−4.7
2013	−20.8	1.0	−8.0	10.0	−18.8
2014	−16.0	1.0		14.0	−2.0

Figures in million Euros

Looking Ahead

When Tuenti announced that the company would be gradually discontinuing its social network, trying to focus its activity on mobile phones, the company disclosed that its plans for the future is to become a leader in virtual mobile phones, expanding its activities in South America.

Whether Tuenti will be able to do this or not will be seen in the coming years.

At the beginning of 2016, we can only estimate the economic value that Tuenti should have by now in order not to destroy value for Telefónica. Assuming that in 2015 Tuenti had a similar impact on Telefónica as in 2014, Tuenti should now have a value of €172.2 million (see Table 4.11).

This is no easy task.

Buying a Complementary Business: LinkedIn and Lynda.com

In April 2015, LinkedIn announced the acquisition of Lynda.com, a platform dedicated to online education. The deal was closed at a price of $1,500 million, with 52% paid in cash and the rest in shares. The news had a major media impact because this was LinkedIn's biggest purchase to date. In 2012 the company had bought Slideshare.net and in 2013 Pulse, paying much lower prices – in the range of some hundred million.

Lynda.com was founded in 1995 by Lynda Weinman as a web-based training site that specialized in computer software instruction. The company charged a monthly fee to subscribers who were then permitted to take any training program they wanted. Initially, Lynda.com was the most popular computer skills educational site online, offering tens of thousands of straightforward and comprehensive instructional videos. In 2015 Lynda.com's revenue was $150 million, so LinkedIn paid ten times that.

Table 4.11 Estimated EV of Tuenti at the end of 2015 if value in Telefónica is not to be destroyed

Years		2010	2011	2012	2013	2014	2015
Differential FCF	−70.0	−9.0	−10.5	−4.7	−18.8	−2.0	−2.0
TV							172.2
Total differential FCF	−70.0	−9.0	−10.5	−4.7	−18.8	−2.0	170.2
PV	0.0						

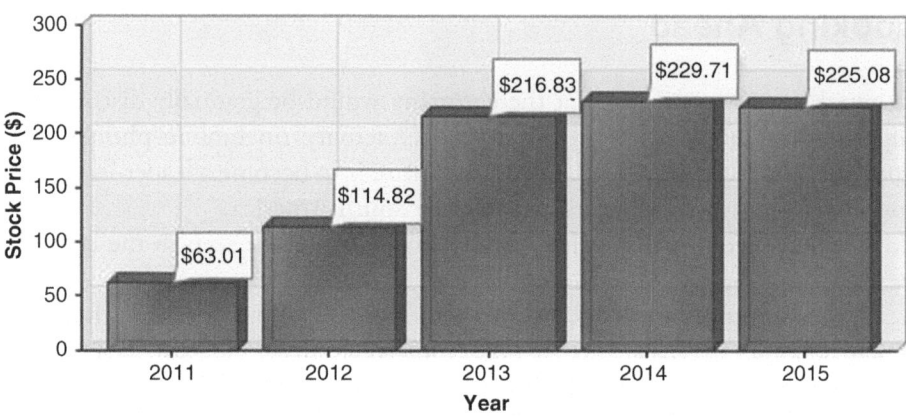

Fig. 4.3 Evolution of LinkedIn's stock price

LinkedIn was founded in December 2002 and launched in May 2003 as a professional network. In October 2008 the company had more than 25 million registered users working in 150 industries. In March 2013 the number of registered users was 200 million, working in more than 200 countries and in all the Fortune 500's biggest companies.

In May 2011 LinkedIn became the first American social network to launch an IPO. The initial price was $45 per share, and the price underwent considerable revaluation over the coming years (see Fig. 4.3).

Did the Price Make Sense?

There was a general consensus about the strategic importance of this operation for LinkedIn, which was interested in obtaining platforms with professional content. There were also some doubts about the price and the way in which new customers would be monetized, since Lynda.com typically was offering relatively cheap courses, costing around $300 per year, and its revenue came from subscriptions.

How can we analyze if a price of $1,500 million for Lynda.com makes economic sense?

Applying our model of intrinsic economic value, this price will only make sense if LinkedIn is able to generate enough differential FCF to compensate for it. In 2014 Lynda.com lost around $62.5 million, with a recurrent operational profit of $15 million. If this were the case, LinkedIn purchased

Lynda.com for a price/earnings ratio (P/E) of around 100 times. And with its sustainable operational profit of $15 million, Lynda.com was not generating positive FCF because of the investments required.

What about the expected growth of the company? Lynda.com's business model enabled significant growth in revenue (34% in 2013; 27% in 2014; 25% in Q1 2015), but also brought considerable increases in admin sales and marketing expenses (from 26% in 2012 to 37% in Q1 2015). Synergies from economies of scale are difficult to obtain.

On the other hand, since both LinkedIn and Lynda.com were apparently targeting a similar group of people, the ideal situation would be for LinkedIn to use this acquisition to coax Lynda.com users to sign up for premium packages.

In fact, these expected synergies haven't shown up, because the typical profile of a LinkedIn user is an educated professional, with high/medium income, who is seeking specialized professional and value creative training. Lynda.com offers middle courses for middle managers and young people, with no grading. Accordingly, traditional LinkedIn users are not interested in the traditional courses of Lynda.com.

Once more, the expected differential FCF associated with the purchase of Lynda.com didn't show up. The so-called MOOC business model of Lynda.com (massive open online courses) was good to build up a brand, but not to generate income and FCF.

What Happened?

At the beginning of February 2016, LinkedIn made public its results for the last quarter of 2015 and for the whole year. The company announced a loss of $8.4 million in the last quarter of 2015 and of $166.1 million for 2015, below the expectations of market analysts. Although revenue increased by 34% in relation to 2014, losses went up ten times, owing to major increases in costs and expenses (see Table 4.12 for more detailed information).

In the first half of February 2016, the share price went down from $150 to $100, reflecting the market's negative view about the future of LinkedIn owing to its lack of capability when it came to monetizing new customers associated with its latest purchases, including Lynda.com, and to control the

Table 4.12 Selected financial information of LinkedIn

Years	2012	2013	2014	2015
Revenue	972.31	1,530.00	2,220.00	2,990.00
Gross margin from operations	846.79	1,330.00	1,940.00	2,640.00
Net income from operations	21.61	26.77	−15.32	−164.76
Cash and equivalent	270.41	803.09	460.89	546.24
Total net assets	1,380.00	3,350.00	5,430.00	7,010.00
Total debt	0.00	0.00	1,080.00	1,130.00
Total equity	908.42	2,630.00	3,330.00	4,470.00

Source: LinkedIn

increase in expenses coming from its expansion in emerging markets, for example China and some African countries.

Lessons from this Operation

Let's summarize some lessons we can learn:

1. Be sure that complementary businesses will offer real synergies. Consider both positive and negative synergies.
2. Identify actions to materialize those synergies. Quantify the economic impact of them.
3. Do not undervalue the competition's answer to your value proposal.
4. Do not underestimate associated costs needed to implement expected synergies.
5. Adjust your offered acquisition's price to a conservative expected future, never to an optimistic one.

Microsoft Comes to the Rescue

On June 13, 2016 many investors were surprised by the announcement that Microsoft was buying LinkedIn for around $26.2 billion, net of cash.

Microsoft was paying $196 per share in cash to acquire LinkedIn, a substantial premium for a stock that closed on Friday, June 10 at $131, and this included about $17 in net cash as of LinkedIn's latest quarter. Additionally, LinkedIn shares had traded as low as $98.25 earlier in 2016 after a huge earnings report. Microsoft was giving close to a 50% premium for a stock that had rallied more than 30% from its lowest point, which had been seen just a few months before June 2016.

Does the Acquisition Make Sense?

As with similar operations, this acquisition made a lot of sense from an operational and strategic point of view.

Microsoft was the largest player in the enterprise software space and, by buying LinkedIn, it would gain entry into the enterprise recruiting, learning and development space (with Lynda.com), as well as, most clearly, professional social networking, a space the company had struggled to enter previously. Additionally, Microsoft's customer relationship management system, Dynamics, had potential integrations with Recruiter, and the integrations between Office 365 offerings and the LinkedIn social network were also appealing.

CEO Satya Nadella wrote a letter to his employees pointing out that, above all, he was looking at the LinkedIn acquisition as a way to "reinvent productivity and business processes." In other words, the deal was an attempt at vertically integrating workplace solutions by being present at the many different stages of the professional cycle.

As D.M. Martins Research commented:

At an individual level, it starts with pre-professional networking and the job search, areas in which LinkedIn has been dominant as the leading professional network platform for a while now. But then it continues with professional development, through LinkedIn's Lynda and, most importantly, with the integration of productivity tools, including Microsoft's Office, SharePoint and Skype. A sales representative at Company XYZ, for example, who originally found his or her job through LinkedIn, could not only generate sales leads through the same platform, but also manage calendar (MS Office), meetings (Skype), and share documents (SharePoint) more seamlessly, provided that the many tools are properly integrated, without ever having to leave the Microsoft umbrella of products and services – all with a single sign on. In the end, the hypothetical salesperson could very well have an all-Microsoft experience in the office, from 9 a.m. to 5 p.m., and never have to seek (or encourage his or her employer to seek) workplace productivity solutions elsewhere.

At the enterprise level, LinkedIn's platform could not only serve as the recruiting tool that it already is, but it could also combine with Microsoft's ERP (enterprise resource planning) system, MS Dynamics, to allow clients to better manage their employee and client databases.

Table 4.13 Selected opinions about Microsoft's LinkedIn acquisition

- It's a good day to be a LinkedIn shareholder – 26.3%
- This move will boost Microsoft's enterprise platform – 19.1%
- That's a hefty price for LinkedIn, but worth it – 7.7%
- The deal may change the social media landscape – 6.9%
- Not sure I see the synergies in this deal – 18.9%
- Microsoft overpaid – not a good move for the company – 21.1%

According to Microsoft CEO Satya Nadella, the combined company's addressable market will climb 58% following the acquisition.

Still, the reaction of the market was that Microsoft was overpaying for LinkedIn. In fact, the price of the LinkedIn shares jumped the same day to the level of the offer, and Microsoft lost 3%.

In a poll conducted by Seeking Alpha, there was a consensus about this point (see Table 4.13).

The Small Detail of the Price

Since the accounting value of the equity of LinkedIn was $4.6 billion, Microsoft was paying a goodwill of $21.6 billion. As we know, this price would only make sense if LinkedIn will generate enough and differential FCF for Microsoft in a foreseeable future. Many Microsoft shareholders were angry with the eventual closing price, which ended up being more than 50% more than the previous Friday close price.

LinkedIn was seeing operating losses ($165 million in 2015 and $45.8 million in Q1 of 2016), with a generation of FCF of around $450 million. Once more, what differential FCF should LinkedIn generate for Microsoft to compensate for a price of $26.2 billion? Where are the positive synergies coming from this acquisition, especially if LinkedIn remains as an independent business unit? Could Microsoft provide the big leadership needed to monetize the extended user base of LinkedIn?

The price to FCF ratio was over 58 times. And the price earnings ratio to growth (PEG) was the higher of its peers (see Table 4.14).

In terms of FCF required in the coming years, Table 4.15 shows a base scenario. According to this analysis, to evaluate the equity of LinkedIn at $33.5 billion, we have to assume that:

1. Differential FCF in next five years will start at $0.5 billion and will finish at $2 billion.

Table **4.14** Some comparable ratios

| | 5 LARGEST TECH NAMES, BY MARKET CAP | | | | | OTHER PEERS | | |
	AAPL	GOOG	New MSFT *	AMZN	FB	LNKD *	TSLA	TWTR
Market cap (bill.)	$536.6	$496.2	$392.3	$339.3	$328.3	$25.6	$32.1	$11.4
Stock price	$97.99	$722.50	$50.00	$720.27	$114.80	$191.40	$220.48	$16.32
2016 EPS	$8.28	$33.60	$2.67	$5.39	$3.55	$3.45	$0.78	$0.52
2017 EPS	$9.11	$39.65	$2.89	$9.92	$4.61	$4.26	$3.33	$0.68
Growth	10.0%	18.0%	8.2%	84.0%	29.9%	23.5%	326.9%	30.8%
2016 P/E	11.8	21.5	18.7	133.6	32.3	55.5	282.7	31.4
PEG	1.18	1.19	2.27	1.59	1.08	2.36	0.86	1.02
Net cash/share	($4.49)	$98.80	$4.20	$16.22	$6.45	$13.45	($18. 22)	$3.01
Cash-adjusted P/E	12.4	18.6	17.2	130.6	30.5	51.6	306.0	25.6
Cash-adjusted PEG	1.23	1.03	2.08	1.55	1.02	2.20	0.94	0.83

Source: DM Martins Research, using data from company reports and press releases
EPS: earnings per share
* estimates are consensus, non-GAAP

Table 4.15 An evaluation of LinkedIn based on DFC

Years		1	2	3	4	5
FCF		0.5	0.8	1.0	1.3	2.0
TV						44.8
Total		0.5	0.8	1.0	1.3	46.8
EV	34.7					
D	1.2					
E	33.5					
TV	44.8					
FCFb	1.5					
g	4.5%					
WACC	8.0%					

2. TV based on a FCF of $1.5 billion will need a permanent growth rate of 4.5%.
3. WACC of LinkedIn will be 8%.

Additionally, the market was surprised with the announcement that Microsoft would finance this acquisition with debt, when the company had more than $100 billion in cash.

Not surprisingly, on June 14 Moody's placed Microsoft's AAA credit rating under review for downgrade, citing concerns that the acquisition would be funded through new debt when the company had enough cash to buy LinkedIn four times over.

The question remains whether this deal will provide enough synergies and data connections to ensure the purchase price was warranted.

On the positive side, we can believe that over time it will, as the LinkedIn platform should turn out to be a perfect fit for Microsoft's suite of products. Traffic is king online and LinkedIn has plenty of it, which can most definitely be monetized much better than at present. Is the deal a risk? Yes – but the combination of these two companies should create plenty of synergies that increase engagement levels over time. If user growth can reaccelerate and engagement levels improve, then revenue growth will undoubtedly come back; and Microsoft knows this. We will see how things play out.

On the negative side, we can consider a pattern that has evolved over the years: the larger the acquisition, the more likely it is to fail. This is in line with Microsoft's own past failures: Skype, Yammer and aQuantative. Microsoft paid $8.5 billion for Skype in 2011, and now it does not show up in its earnings releases at all. Yammer has also never been mentioned again, and aQuantative was almost completely written off after Microsoft bought it for $6.5 billion.

For those who are less optimistic, LinkedIn does not seem to be a high-quality business. Up to now, it has made its money from premium subscriptions and advertising, but the majority of its revenue comes from talent solutions or from recruiting. Essentially, LinkedIn is a large repository for computerized résumés. A big question mark hangs over whether Microsoft will be able to change this business model.

The Value of Data

In mid-February 2016, IBM announced the acquisition of Truven Health Analytics Inc. (THA) for $2.6 billion, in a bid to expand its already considerable presence in the health-care industry. THA, based in Ann Arbor, Michigan, supplies healthcare data services to employers, hospitals and drug-makers to help them gauge the efficacy of products and services. Its software can scan millions of records and, for example, tell employers or hospitals whether patients were given unnecessary procedures.

THA is one of relatively few companies with a large collection of commercial claims, which reflect what medical-services insurers actually pay for on behalf of members and how much they spend. Such data is vital as employers, insurers, health-care providers and others try to track patterns of spending, identify gaps in care and shift to new forms of payment that are intended to reward efficiency and quality.

The deal would double the size of IBM's Watson Health business unit to 5,000 employees, as the company added new technology services to sell to doctors and hospitals. IBM had been on a healthcare spending spree over the past few years, doling out more than $4 billion to buy medical technology companies.

IBM's other health-care acquisitions included Phytel Inc. and Explorys Inc., companies that maintained clinical data on more than 50 million patients, and Merge Healthcare Inc., which specialized in medical image technology. IBM had folded these acquisitions into Watson Health, aiming to develop software to analyze vast amounts of data and make suggestions that doctors could use to improve medical care.

With THA, as with several other recent IBM acquisitions, the prize was data, which IBM would use to improve its Watson artificial-intelligence system. Machine-learning systems such as Watson required immense amounts of so-called training data, from which useful patterns are extracted.

THA was formerly the health-care unit of Thomson Reuters Corp. It was sold in 2012 to private-equity firm Veritas Capital Fund Management LLC for $1.25 billion. In March 2016, Veritas failed to make an IPO of THA at an estimated EV of $3 billion.

Once more, THA's acquisition by IBM was considered a reasonable strategic movement which makes a lot of sense. As always, the question mark was not the operation but the price. Was IBM overvaluing THA when it paid $2.6 billion for the company? How can we evaluate an intangible asset such as data?

Evaluating Truven Health Analytics, Inc.

In terms of extrinsic value, to pay $2.6 billion for THA means to evaluate it at an EV/EBITDA of 20, since we can consider that EBITDA is similar to FCF from operations (taxes are 0). This ratio was in line with some multiples of the market at that time. For example, in March 2015, Inovalon Holdings Inc., a company that sells data analytics that can be used to cut costs in the healthcare industry, made an IPO of $600 million with an implicit EV/earnings before interest, taxes, depreciation and amortization (EBITDA) of 40.

Still, to double check whether the market at that time was overvaluing companies, we have to understand the implicit assumptions related to the intrinsic valuation of THA.

Table 4.16 shows some selected financial information about THA.

In terms of intrinsic EV, we can see that in 2015 THA was expected to generate a positive FCF, but without new investments in capital expenditure. If we consider an average need in new investments of $50 million, then the sustainable and comparable FCF of THA in 2015 was negative.

Table 4.16 THA. Inc. Some financial information

Years	2013	2014	2015
Revenues	492.7	544.5	600.0
EBIaT	7.4	10.8	10.0
Depreciation	87.6	106.5	120.0
FCF from operations	95.0	117.3	130.0
FCF from operating working capital	−96.4	−72.1	−80.0
Capital expenditure	−44.0	−142.1	−40.0
Total FCF	−45.4	−96.9	10.0
Debt	872.0	977.0	975.0

Figures in millions of US $

So, a first point is to understand how IBM is going to use the data acquired with THA in order to monetize this information for its old and new customers, generating differential and sustainable positive FCF.

In any case, if IBM paid $2.6 billion for THA it is because it considered that the acquired company had a higher value. Assuming that the estimated EV was around $3 billion, and that this EV can be estimated with an extrapolation of a FCF, growing at a particular rate forever, to understand this price we can analyze:

1. The needed differential and sustainable FCF THA has to generate for IBM, under reasonable assumptions about the WACC and the growth rate.
2. The needed differential and sustainable growth rate of THA based on a reasonable differential and sustainable FCF for IBM, and with a reasonable WACC.

In Table 4.17 we summarize this analysis.
To estimate the required FCF that has to be extrapolated in order to have an EV of $3,000 million, we assumed that a sustainable and reasonable growth rate will be 3% and that the WACC is 10%. The needed FCF is $233 million.

To estimate the growth rate required to have an EV of $3,000 million, we assumed that a reasonable and sustainable FCF would be $20 million with the same WACC of 10%. The growth rate required is 9.27%.

Both figures, the needed FCF and the required growth rate, do not seem very realistic.

This is the same conclusion we can reach if we try to estimate the EV by assuming some expected reasonable and differential FCF for a period of, say, five years, in line with the previous cases.

With a WACC of 10% and some FCF going from 10 to 100 in five years, the TV required to have an EV of 3,000 implies a growth rate of 7.63%, which is totally unrealistic (see Table 4.18).

Table 4.17 Evaluating some key factors in EV

Analyzing Key Value Factors (KVF) in EV of THA			
Needed FCF when:	233	Needed g when:	9.3%
growth rate	3.0%	Expected FCF	20
WACC	10.0%	WACC	10.0%
In order to have		In order to have	
EV	3,000	EV	3,000

Table 4.18 Evaluation

Years		1	2	3	4	5
FCF		10	20	50	75	100
TV						4,547
		10	20	50	75	4,647
EV	3,000					
g	7.63%					
WACC	10.00%					

Finally, in terms of a real option, we can consider that, by buying THA, IBM was buying an option to sell THA in five years at an estimated price. In this case, we should analyze the value of this real option to understand whether the $2,600 million paid makes sense. Technically, we should analyze a reasonable value of a put option on the shares of THA in 1 year. Under what circumstances and assumptions would it make sense to evaluate this option at $1,600 million?[3]

To calculate this value we can use the Black Scholes formula, considering the value of buying a European put option, at one year, with the following characteristics:

• Value of the underlying asset	• $2,000 million
• Exercise price	• $3,046 million
• Volatility of the underlying asset	• 50%
• Time	• five years
• Risk free rate	• 4%

Note that we are keeping similar assumptions about the present estimated economic value of the equity of THA ($2,000 million) and in the needed TV in five years, as noted above. Under these assumptions, the value of this option would be $1,085 million, which indicates an overvaluation of THA at $2,000 million. Following this approach, to pay $2,000 million for the equity of THA only would imply no overvaluation if IBM expected a value of the equity of THA of $4,445 million in five years, if other assumptions remain unchanged.

With the exercise price of $3,046 million, even with a volatility of 100% of the share price of THA, the value of the option would be below the $2,000 million (see Table 4.16 and Fig. 4.4), which reinforces the idea of an overvaluation (Table 4.19).

---

[3] We assume that E = EV – Debt; and Debt is 1,000.

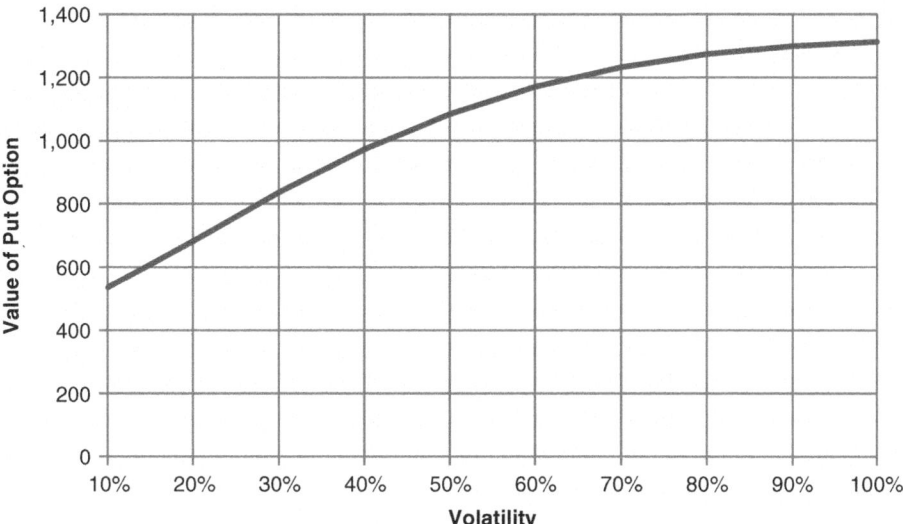

Fig. 4.4 Volatility of the underlying asset and expected value of the option

Table 4.19 Volatility of the underlying asset and expected value of the option

Volatility	Expected value
50%	1,085
10%	536
20%	682
30%	836
40%	973
50%	1,085
60%	1,171
70%	1,232
80%	1,274
90%	1,299
100%	1,312

Summary

Let's summarize some conclusions that can be drawn from the analysis made in this chapter:

1. For any extrinsic valuation, try to understand the influence of short-term (speculative) movements on the market value.
2. Decide the type of investor you want to be: short term, speculative; long term, looking for sustainable value.

3. Estimate the sustainability of the market price based on a reasonable intrinsic valuation.
4. Select a key value driver (KVD) and determine how reasonable the assumptions are that you require in order to get the present market value.
5. Be aware of the type of share you are buying, in terms of liquidity, control and rights.
6. Be sure that complementary business will offer real synergies. Consider both positive and negative synergies.
7. Identify actions to materialize those synergies. Quantify the economic impact of them.
8. Do not undervalue competition's answer to your value proposal.
9. Do not underestimate associated costs to implement expected synergies.
10. Adjust your offered acquisition price to a conservative expected future, never to an optimistic one.

5

Managing to Deliver Value in a Digital World

Introduction

In previous chapters we have discussed the new digital economy – an economy that is based on digital technologies-, its main components and new digital business models. We have also set up the fundamentals to understand what economic value (EV) is. And we have discussed how and when these business models can create EV, analyzing business decisions taken by some digital companies.

In this chapter we will take a more general approach, with the objective of discussing the key points to be considered in order to manage in a digital economy, while trying to deliver EV.

Some Comments About Revenue Models

In Chapter 1 we defined some digital business models from the point of view of how they can generate revenue. After the analysis that followed, we can now summarize some points about these revenue models and their generation of EV.

Freemium model. This business model is supposed to be free for 90% of its users and to generate revenue on the remaining 10%, based on fees for additional services. A typical example of a freemium model is LinkedIn.

© The Author(s) 2017
F. J. López Lubián, J. Esteves, *Value in a Digital World*,
DOI 10.1007/978-3-319-51750-6_5

As noted, the big challenge for freemium models is generating enough revenue to cover expenses, eliminating losses. In most of the cases, either revenue is lower than expenses, or payments from customers are very poor. In other cases, revenue is very irregular because customers become interested only when they need an offered service, as in LinkedIn's revenue from job offers. This introduces a volatility to the cash flows which increases the operational risk of the business model. So far, eventual additional revenue coming from advertising has been insufficient to moderate losses and volatility.

Advertising model. In this model, revenue comes from advertising and, consequently, the number of users is a key metric to evaluate its EV. As already noted in previous chapters, the relevant information is not just the total number of users, but the number of users who are differential in terms of revenue from advertising. Since advertising expenses follow users, not companies, the increase in the number of competitors tends to decrease a company's revenue from advertising, putting in danger the profitability of this business model. Additionally, there is a limit to the amount of publicity a single user can receive. The case of Twitter is a good example of this tendency.

Community model. An example of this model is Instagram. Revenue is very unstable because it depends on whether the site is fashionable or not.

Infomediary model. In this revenue model, affiliate programs offer products and services that website visitors will probably be interested in purchasing, or the company holds data which are very valuable for a potential customer. For example, Amazon has developed an extensive affiliate program by helping individual websites link to specific products that Amazon offers. An affiliate often recommends or reviews products, and posts that information on the Amazon site. Revenue coming from this model is always limited by the interest in and availability of the associated data.

In any case, to measure the EV generated by any business model, we have to consider not only the expected revenue but also:

1. The total free cash flow (FCF), which includes costs, expenses and investments needed to make the business sustainable.
2. The associated capital structure to finance the company.

Delivering Value to Business Stakeholders

For any company, whether operating in a digital world or not, the best way to deliver EV to business stakeholders is to implement business policies that allow that company to be sustainable and that allow it to create EV not only for the company, but also for its stakeholders.

A useful way to look at any company is to separate its operational aspects from its financial aspects. In graphical terms, and applying the methodology of EV discussed in this book, we can see that all the elements included in FCF summarize the operational aspects of a company, while the financial aspects are related to the providers of financing: debt and equity (see Fig. 5.1).

In this context and following this approach, we can also differentiate between stakeholders, who are related to the operational aspects of the company, and stakeholders, who are linked to the financial aspects.

Among the first stakeholders, we find groups such as the workers (both management team and non-management), suppliers, customers and, in general, all the professionals and companies that contribute to the generation of the company's FCF. The stakeholders related to the financial aspects of the company are the suppliers of its financing, basically the financial institutions who provide debt (via its different instruments), the eventual holders of bonds issued by the company and the shareholders of the company who provide the equity (via different kinds of capital).

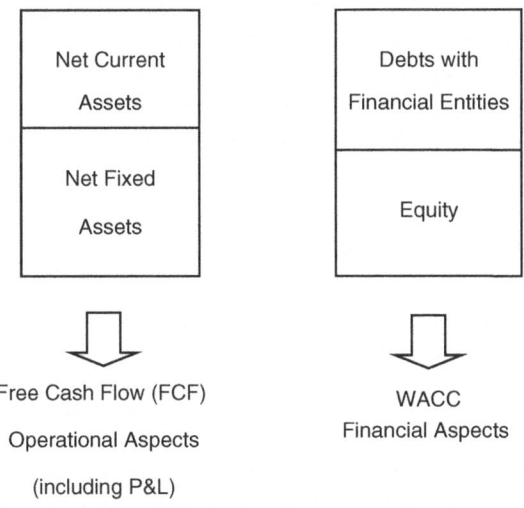

Fig. 5.1 Operational and financial aspects in a company

In order to survive, any company has to be economically feasible and profitable. This means that it has to generate enough FCF to fulfill all the needed payments that become due to its financial resource providers.

Economic feasibility tends to be related to the payments due to financial institutions. In fact, a company is in a situation of financial distress when the company is not generating enough FCF to fulfill the required payments to the debt. If this happens and the company is unable to fix the situation, the only way out is liquidation.

But a company also has to generate FCF to remunerate its shareholders, to give them an economic profitability that compensates for the money they're putting into the company. Otherwise, the company won't survive, because nobody will invest to lose value.

In summary, if a company wants to deliver EV to its business stakeholders, that company has to have business policies and business opportunities that allow it to generate enough sustainable FCF to properly remunerate all its operational and financial stakeholders.

We can therefore conclude:

1. For any company to deliver EV for its stakeholders it's not only a matter of delivering accounting value or accounting profitability. In that sense, it would be incorrect to believe that only accounting metrics, such as return on assets (ROA) or return on equity (ROE), measure the EV.
2. For any company, delivering EV for its stakeholders is a matter of generating differential and sustainable FCF in an amount enough to cover their expected return.
3. If a company has problems in generating this FCF, the solution is not to increase the total FCF by decreasing the required FCF for the operational stakeholders. The solution should be to implement changes (if possible) to better manage all the operational policies of the company in order to increase the generation of FCF.

An example will help us to visualize these ideas.

Let's consider the case of CVP, a company operating in the Real Estate Industry.

How can we know if CVP delivers EV to its stakeholders? We know that this EV is not only a matter of accounting metrics, such as revenue, gross margin, earnings before interest and taxes, ROA or ROE. It's a matter of understanding how CVP generates FCF, in terms of where this FCF is coming from, and where this FCF is going to.

Let's assume that CVP generates a sustainable and consistent FCF of 500, broken down as follows:

FCF from operations	1,000
FCF from operational working capital (OWC)	−100
FCF from capital expenditure	−400
Total FCF	500

This total FCF of 500 goes to cover the service of debt and to remunerate its shareholders, as follows:

Total FCF	500
To cover service of debt	−400
To shareholders	−100

Let's also assume that this FCF is enough to properly remunerate all CVP's operational and financial stakeholders.

This means that behind this sustainable operational FCF of 1,000, CVP has a sustainable profit and loss (P&L) where all the professionals and companies contributing to generate this FCF are properly remunerated: workers have a competitive salary (including fringe benefits), linked to their contribution to the generation of EV; suppliers have contracts at prices and economic conditions in line with the quality of the products or services offered; customers are satisfied with the price in relation to quality, and they remain loyal because the offer of CVP is better than the competition's.

This also means that behind this sustainable FCF from Operational working capital (OWC) of −100, CVP has agreed collection policies with customers and inventory management policies and payment policies with suppliers in line with market conditions and with the expected FCF of these customers and suppliers.

Finally, by investing 400 CVP is wisely ensuring its future, maintaining the value of its fixed assets and incorporating new assets in order to keep the company's present competitive advantages.

As noted above, this FCF of 500 is dedicated to remunerate CVP's finance providers. The company has a reasonable and sustainable capital structure with reasonable and sustainable costs of debt and equity. This expected profitability of debt and equity is fully covered with the 400 and 100 dedicated to them. CVP is economically sustainable and profitable, since it generates enough FCF to service its debt, and to give an economic profitability to its shareholders above the minimum expected cost of equity.

What happens if, for whatever reason, CVP is not able to maintain this FCF of 500?

Since the company will still need the 500 to remunerate equity and debt, the solution is not to generate the required 500 by unilaterally destroying value for its operational stakeholders – for example, by reducing required operational expenses, workers' salaries without any negotiation, delaying the payments to suppliers with no compensation or delaying required investment in fixed assets. These can be partial and temporary answers to the lack of cash flow, but not permanent solutions.

Any permanent solution will include an understanding of why and where the company is losing its capacity to generate a FCF of 500 through maintaining the old conditions for the operational stakeholders. Does this loss come from the FCF from operations? Or does it come from the FCF from OWC? Can we adjust our investment policy without losing opportunities for future growth?

For example, if this loss comes from a decline in the P&L, CVP's management should try to introduce new policies to replace the lack of FCF: for example, finding new markets, new products, new pricing policy; increasing efficiency; implementing better cost control.

On the other hand, if after careful analysis CVP's management team believes that in future CVP won't be able to maintain the old generation of FCF, they should renegotiate the distribution of a new and reduced FCF with the operational and financial stakeholders of CVP.

In any case, we have to keep in mind that to measure the economic profitability of any stakeholder we have to use the appropriate tool. As previously noted, this is not only a matter of accounting profitability, but refers to the internal rate of returns of differential cash flows.

Does Digital Business Cannibalization Matter?

In any quantification of EV and/or economic profitability associated with a business decision, the hard part is to determine whether a cash flow is differential or not. This could be especially difficult in digital businesses, where innovation is a key factor to generate EV.

Consider the case of the erosion or cannibalization that is generated during the launch of a new product or service. In the analysis of the economic profitability associated with the decision to launch a new product, a key factor is the expected market share that the new product will achieve. In digital business, new products and services tend to replace existing ones, offering new versions with more operational capabilities.

In this context, let's consider the case of a digital company planning to launch a new product (B). The company already has in the market a product (A), and the management team is aware that part of the sales of the new product will cannibalize product A's existing sales.

Does this company have to consider this cannibalization effect in the EV analysis of the launch of product B?

The conceptual answer is yes, if only for the differential FCFs associated with the launching of product B.

Let's assume that the investment analysis for the launch of product B excluding the eventual erosion in product A is the following:

Years		1	2	3	4	5
FCF		−4,500	1,500	1,750	2,000	2,100	3,000
Weighted average cost of capital (WACC)	8%					
Net present value (NPV)	3,562					

We go to the marketing department of the company, and we ask for the estimated loss in sales of product A after the launch of product B. Since we already know the estimated FCF generated for product A, we can estimate the lost FCF in the company caused by the launch of product B, assuming that all the losses in sales of A are differential, meaning that they will happen because of the launch of B, and only because of this launch.

The numerical analysis will be:

Years	1	2	3	4	5
Revenue	15,000	10,000	8,000	4,000	2,000
FCF as percentage of sales	12%	12%	12%	12%	12%
FCF lost	1,800	1,200	960	480	240

Of course, if all these lost FCFs are differential, then the combined effect of launching product B will be the FCF generated by B plus the FCF lost because of the launch of B, as follows:

Years		1	2	3	4	5
FCF	−4,500	−300	550	1,040	1,620	2,760
WACC	8%					
NPV	−411					

If this were the case, the decision should be to not launch product B.

In any case, before implementing this decision we have to be sure that all the FCF lost by product A will be differential. This means that the loss will be created only by the company, as a consequence of the launch of product B, independently of the actions of the company's competitors.

As far as this digital company is operating in a global and competitive economy, where innovation matters, it can be very unrealistic to assume that the erosion in sales of product A, as a consequence of launching product B, will be provoked only by the company.

How can we be sure that we are considering only the differential FCF? One way is to ask the right questions.

In fact, the right question to ask the marketing department is not about the estimated losses of sales of product A because of the launch of product B, but about the estimated differential losses associated with this decision.

The estimated differential losses will be:

> The loss in sales of product A because product B is launched, not taking into account the action of the competition;
>
> minus
>
> The net loss in sales of product A provoked by the action of the competition, as a consequence of launching product B versus not launching product B.

In this example, we can perceive different situations. For example, in Table 5.1 we have one possible numerical analysis, when all the erosion is not fully provoked by the company.

In this case, the differential FCF to be considered in the decision will be the FCF of the project without erosion minus the net FCF created by the erosion:

Years		1	2	3	4	5
FCF	−4,500	900	1,150	1,400	1,860	2,880
WACC	8%					
NPV	1,758					

According to this analysis, the decision will be to launch product B.

Note that in some cases the net effect of the erosion can produce positive differential FCFs. This would be the case if we launched product B in order to compensate a higher cannibalization of A that is coming from the competition, as summarized in Table 5.2.

Table 5.1 Erosion not fully provoked by the company

Estimated losses of revenue in product A owing to the launch of product B, not taking into account the action of the competence

Years	1	2	3	4	5
Revenue	15,000	10,000	8,000	4,000	2,000
FCF as percentage of sales	12%	12%	12%	12%	12%
FCF lost	1,800	1,200	960	480	240

Estimated net losses of revenue from product A owing to the action of the competition after the launch of product B versus the alternative of not launching B

Years	1	2	3	4	5
Revenue	10,000	5,000	3,000	2,000	1,000
FCF as percentage of sales	12%	12%	12%	12%	12%
FCF lost	1,200	600	360	240	120
Net effect of the erosion					

Years	1	2	3	4	5
Revenue	5,000	5,000	5,000	2,000	1,000
FCF as percentage of sales	12%	12%	12%	12%	12%
FCF lost	600	600	600	240	120
Differential FCF	−600	−600	−600	−240	−120

Table 5.2 Avoiding a higher cannibalization

Estimated losses of revenue in product A owing to the launch of product B, not taking into account the action of the competence

Years	1	2	3	4	5
Revenue	15,000	10,000	8,000	4,000	2,000
FCF as percentage of Sales	12%	12%	12%	12%	12%
FCF lost	1,800	1,200	960	480	240

Estimated net losses of revenue in product A owing to the action of the competition after the launch of product B versus not launching B

Years	1	2	3	4	5
Revenue	16,000	12,000	8,500	4,000	2,000
FCF as percentage of sales	12%	12%	12%	12%	12%
FCF lost	1,920	1,440	1,020	480	240
Net effect of the erosion					

Years	1	2	3	4	5
Revenue	−1,000	−2,000	−500	0	0
FCF as percentage of sales	12%	12%	12%	12%	12%
FCF lost	−120	−240	−60	0	0
Differential FCF	120	240	60	0	0

In this case, the differential FCF to be considered will be the FCF of the project without erosion minus the net FCF created by the erosion:

| Estimated FCF of the launch including erosion | | | | | |
Years	1	2	3	4	5
FCF	−4,500	1,620	1,990	2,060	2,100	3,000
WACC	8%
NPV	3,927

Now the EV creation of launching product B will be even higher, because through its launch we are delaying a cannibalization of A by competitors.

In conclusion, the erosion effect has to be considered. In some cases, this effect can be positive in terms of differential FCF. This tends to be the case in digital business, where innovation and competition are key factors in creating EV.

IT Investments

Since innovation is one key characteristic in a digital economy, IT investment in digital business can be provoked by new technologies which replace existing and fully operational ones. Do managers have to invest in new technologies in order to use state-of-the-art technologies when the present one is operational and is expected to be operational in the future? How to deal with this situation? Which are the differential FCFs that should be included in the economic analysis?

Let's consider the case of Optiplus, a company operating in the telecoms industry.

Optiplus management was considering the possibility of replacing a machine, IS9, with a new one, IS10, which incorporates more advanced technology. A summary of the main characteristics of the two machines is as follows:

MODEL IS9: CURRENT MACHINE
Cost €100,000 five years ago.
Has depreciated by the straight-line method over ten years.
Has five years' useful life remaining. It works perfectly.
Could be sold today for €30,000.
Five years from now the market value of the machine will be €0.
In five years the working capital will be liquidated at book value.

REPLACING IS9 WITH IS10, WITH NEW TECHNOLOGY
Cost of investment €200,000.
Will reduce operating costs by €41,500 a year.
Will be depreciated (straight-line method) over eight years.
In five years it could be sold for €50,000.

Replacing the machine will not increase sales, but it will reduce working capital requirements by €5,000 in the first year.

In five years the working capital will be liquidated at book value.

Assuming that Optiplus has a tax rate of 30%, and that the rate of discount to be used for both alternatives is 10%, Table 5.3 includes the differential FCF associated with this management decision and the differential EV.

Note that from Year 1 to Year 5 the differential depreciation is €15,000, since the yearly depreciation of the new model is €25,000 and the lost depreciation from the present model is €10,000.

Additionally, selling IS9 now will generate a loss of €20,000 (difference between the net book value and the market value). This loss will generate a differential tax saving of €6,000.

For the same reason, in Year 5 the sale of IS10 will generate a loss of €25,000. This loss will generate a differential tax saving of €7,500.

Table 5.3 Analysis of the EVC

Differential Cash Flows from Operations	Initial	YEAR 1	YEARS 2–4	YEAR 5
SAVING OF OPERATING COSTS		41,500	41,500	41,500
DIFFERENTIAL DEPRECIATION		−15,000	−15,000	−15,000
DIFFERENTIAL earnings before interest and taxes		26,500	26,500	26,500
TAXES		−7,950	−7,950	−7,950
DIFFERENTIAL earnings before interest and after taxes		18,550	18,550	18,550
DIFFERENTIAL operational cash flow		33,550	33,550	33,550
Differential Cash Flows from OWC				
SAVING IN WORLING CAPITAL		5,000		−5,000
Differential Cash Flows from Capital Expenditure				
PURCHASE OF NEW MACHINE	−200,000			
SALE OF EXISTING MACHINE	30,000			
FISCAL SAVINGS FOR LOSS	6,000			
SALE OF NEW MACHINE				50,000
TAX SAVING FOR LOSS				7,500
Total cash flow from capital expenditure	−164,000			57,500
Total Differential Cash Flows				
Differential cash Flows from operations	0	33,550	33,550	33,550
Differential cash flows from OWC	0	5,000	0	−5,000
Differential cash flows from capital expenditure	−164,000	0	0	57,500
Total Differential FCF	−164,000	38,550	33,550	86,050

DIFFERENTIAL CASH FLOWS ASSOCIATED WITH IS10 IN RELATION TO KEEPING IS9. Figures in Euros.

Finally, the liquidation in Year 5 of the OWC of IS10 will generate a differential negative cash flow of €5,000, compensating for the reduction of €5,000 in Year 1.

The NPV of these differential FCFs, discounted at 10%, is €325. It's clear that the expected EV created for this replacement is very low, and it can become negative with any minor change in the expected figures.

As usual, we can make a sensitivity analysis on the needed saving in operational costs associated with IS10, to get an economic profitability of, say, 12%. In this case, the saving should be a yearly figure of €45,000.

Impact of Digitization in Business Sustainability

Experiences of the implementation of digitization processes are not always positive. Among other reasons, this is because, for any company, becoming digital has to be linked to its strategy and business sustainability.

In order to avoid pitfalls, it's important to distinguish between digitization and digital transformation.

Digitization is about the digitization of processes, services and products. A typical digitation might offer new services via apps.

Digital transformation is about integrating three main components: products/services, customers and the business model. It's about creating a new business model which reaches new customers, offers new services and products, and generates new differential profits. In any case, the reality of digital transformation suggests that the process requires time to show results. Furthermore, there is a consensus that the process also implies rethinking about the measurement of EV, as previously discussed in this book.

New Trends in Digital

Big Data

Data volumes are exploding, so much so that 90% of the data in the world today was created in the last 10 years.[1] Companies around the world are facing a major problem: they are creating and collecting huge amounts of data that cannot be processed with traditional data analytics tools. Big data

---

[1] Bringing big data to the enterprise, IBM, https://www-01.ibm.com/software/data/bigdata/what-is-big-data.html.

comes in to rescue companies. This is a term used to refer to extremely large or complex data sets which traditional data processing tools are not able to handle. Some of the critical data analytics challenges include data analysis, capture, data curation, search, querying, sharing and data visualization.

Big data can be described in three dimensions (known as the big data three Vs): Velocity, Variety and Volume. Velocity is associated with the speed of data creation, processing, dissemination and visualization. Companies have to deal with the challenge of real time speed of data creation and use. The sheer volume of data is massive, and is doubling in size every two years. Some years ago, this was a major headache, but the decrease in storage costs and better data storage management systems has solved the problem. Not long ago, most of the data created was structured data, in other words it resided in a fixed field within a record or file, and was usually contained in related databases and spreadsheets. Nowadays, some studies show that over 75% of the data created by a company is unstructured (not contained in a database and not organized in a predefined manner). The wide variety of business data (both structured and unstructured) requires a new approach and different techniques for storage and processing.

>Additionally, there are two other dimensions to take into account: veracity and value. Veracity refers to data quality and the issues caused by incorrect data. Therefore, companies need to ensure that both data and analysis of data are correct, particularly in automated decision-making where no human action is involved. Finally, for many people the most important dimension is value. This refers to a firm's ability to convert the four Vs of big data into business value. It demands a carefully designed strategy and an understanding of big data costs and benefits.

Big data investments include technology (big data hardware and software), complementary investments in employee training, analytics skills development and investing in big data talent by recruiting data scientists and experts.

Artificial Intelligence

Nowadays, Artificial Intelligence (AI) is becoming important in the business world, but in reality the concept is not so new. John McCarthy, a Stanford researcher, coined the term in 1956, describing AI as a field which attempts to build intelligent machines and tries to understand intelligent entities.

During the last decade, AI has evolved a lot, especially with new advances in natural language processing (computers are now able to derive meaning from human language) and machine learning (computers are able to learn from data rather than merely respond to human programming). The second age of machine learning is what IBM calls the "cognitive era." This began when Watson, IBM's Big Blue cognitive computing system, won the US game show *Jeopardy*. AI and machine learning are already widely used; for example, Apple's voice recognition service (Siri) and the increasingly reliable Google search results. They are also used for better weather forecasting, stock market high frequency trading and lower levels of spam email in an inbox.

The world has been moving in the direction of cognitive computing for years. Think about autonomous cars, fraud detection systems in banks and complex trading systems that can act faster than human traders. Some business sectors are likely to be affected by AI adoption, such as finance, healthcare, education, infrastructure and utilities, transportation and retail. Some companies have started to appoint chief AI officers, with one eye clearly on the future.

Currently, many investors show a growing interest in companies and startups that are either exposed to or based upon AI technology. Bank of America Merrill Lynch research points out that in 2014 around $2 billion was invested in 322 publicly listed companies of this nature.[2] Some venture capital firms are funding these AI startups from their early stages.

Robotics

The field of robotics has experienced huge evolution over the past decade. The rapid development of robotics and AI is driving us to a new era of growth and innovation fueled by intelligent automation, in which robots will help humans at work and home.

Initially, robots were mainly used for industrial purposes and largely for repetitive tasks, which required speed, strength and moderate precision. With their growing computing power, the development of miniature precision sensors and machine learning, robots are moving from making cars to driving them. The new era of robotics is no longer a concern confined to manufacturing issues, but encompasses the use of robotics in the workplace or at home. New robotics applications have found their place in military, aerial, medical, marketing, retail and consumer service contexts.

Furthermore, the use of virtual robots is growing very fast. These are software programs that build blocks of software inside a computer. Examples are Web crawlers, software programs that perform search tasks on the Web, or chatterbots (also known as chatbots), software programs that conduct

---

[2] Robot Revolution – Global Robot & AI Primer, Bank of America Report, http://www.bofaml.com/content/dam/boamlimages/documents/PDFs/robotics_and_ai_condensed_primer.pdf.

conversations via auditory or textual methods. A promising area is evolutionary robotics, which focuses on the development of automatic methods to create intelligent autonomous robot controllers, without the need for direct programming by humans.

The new robotics industry is growing at a compound rate of 17% a year from more than $71 billion in 2015 to a predicted $135 billion by 2019.[3] Other indicators, such as the number of robotics technology patent filings, show the expected impact of robotics. The main reasons for this growth are the drop in cost of high-quality robots and components, faster computing processors and easier software programming.

Internet of Things

The rise of robotics is possible in part because of the evolution of the Internet of Things (IOT), which is defined as "the internetworking of physical devices, vehicles, buildings and other items—embedded with electronics, software, sensors, actuators, and network connectivity that enable these objects to collect and exchange data."[4] The aim is for the IOT to connect every object (living and non-living) to the Internet and to make them communicate.

The adoption and use of the IOT will give immediate access to real-time data about the physical world and objects within it, which will enable companies to develop new innovative services and solutions, as well as increase business efficiency and productivity. Some of the promising areas for the IOT are smart cities, smart energy, smart homes and smart healthcare.

Nowadays, the world population is estimated at 7.4 billion, with more than half living in cities, and there is an increasing trend of urbanization. Since cities are now becoming more complex and unmanageable in many regions, leaders are looking for new opportunities to improve the quality of life in them, and their efficiency and sustainability. Smart cities seem to be the next big thing in their digital transformation. The development of a smart city infrastructure requires millions of sensors, providing real-time data for analysis. This leads to better and informed decision-making, and provides useful and accurate information to all the citizens. With sensors in place and

---

[3] Worldwide Semiannual Commercial Robotics Spending Guide, IDC report, March 2016, http://www.idc.com/getdoc.jsp?containerId=IDC_P33201.

[4] Internet of Things Global Standards Initiative 2012, http://www.itu.int/ITU-T/recommendations/rec.aspx?rec=y.2060.

interconnectivity established, the possible uses of this information are huge and the opportunities are enormous.[5]

Augmented and Virtual Reality

Augmented reality (AR) technology refers to the superimposition of a digitally generated image or information on a user's existing environment in real time. As a result, AR technology functions by enhancing one's current perception of reality.[6] In contrast to AR, virtual reality (VR) replaces the real world with a completely artificial environment.

In an AR system, the computer or mobile device uses sensors and algorithms to detect the position and orientation of a camera, then sophisticated 3D rendering engines superimpose the computer-generated images onto the user's view of the real world. VR uses similar sensors and algorithms, but in this case the purpose is to locate the user's eyes within the virtual world. VR movement features follow the user's movement and react accordingly in real time. Rather than overlaying images created by computers on a real environment, VR technology generates a convincing and interactive world for the user.

Companies such as Google (Google Glass), Microsoft (Hololens), Samsung (Samsung GearVR), Facebook (Oculus) and HTC (HTC vive) are the most relevant companies in the development of VR devices. In parallel, there are many companies developing controllers, components and software applications around AR and VR.

Summary

1. For any company, to deliver EV for its stakeholders it's not only a matter of delivering accounting value or accounting profitability. In that sense, it would be incorrect to believe that only accounting metrics, such as ROA or ROE, measure EV.
2. For any company, delivering EV for its stakeholders it's a matter of generating differential and sustainable FCF, and in an amount enough to cover their expected return.

---

[5] http://www.itu.int/ITU-T/recommendations/rec.aspx?rec=y.2060.
[6] Graham, M., Zook, M. and Boulton, A. (2013), "Augmented reality in urban places: contested content and the duplicity of code". *Transactions of the Institute of British Geographers*, 38, 464–479.

3. If a company has problems in generating this required FCF, the solution is not to increase the total FCF by decreasing the required FCF for the operational stakeholders. The solution should be to implement changes (if possible) to better manage all the operational policies of the company in order to increase the generation of FCF.

4. The erosion effect has to be considered and, in some cases, this effect can be positive in terms of differential FCF. This tends to be the case in digital business, where innovation and competition are key factors to create EV.

5. Experiences about the implementation of digitization processes are not always positive. Among other reasons, this is because becoming digital has to be linked to a company's strategy and business sustainability.

6. In order to avoid pitfalls, it's important to distinguish between digitization and digital transformation.

7. Digitization is about the digitization of processes, services and products. A typical digitization might offer new services via apps.

8. Digital transformation is about to integrate three main components: products/services, customers and business model. It's about to create a new business model which reaches new customers, offering new services and products and generating differential new profits.

9. New trends in the digital world include topics such as big data, AI, robotics, IOT, AR and VR.

6

Dealing With the Value Perception Gap

Introduction

In this book we have been dealing with the digital economy, digital business and economic valuation. By studying several different companies, we have reviewed different digital business models and analyzed the possibility that they will generate economic value (EV).

Among other conclusions, we have learned that, in order to survive, any business needs to be economically sustainable, which means to be economically feasible and profitable. In other words, economical sustainability implies the generation of economic value.

Applying these concepts to digital business, we can now summarize some critical points to be considered when measuring economic value.

Some Points to be Taken into Account

Point 1: Economic value is not accounting value.

EV is not accounting value, nor sentimental value or any other type of qualitative values. This doesn't mean that other values which are not EV are irrelevant. It means that, to be economically sustainable, the only value that matters is EV.

The economic sustainability of a digital business is not only a matter of generating accounting profit or increasing its accounting value reflected in the total amount of assets. In fact, a business model for a company may be

© The Author(s) 2017
F.J. López Lubián, J. Esteves, *Value in a Digital World*,
DOI 10.1007/978-3-319-51750-6_6

generating accounting profit and increasing its accounting value, but it may be destroying EV and leading the company to an unsustainable situation.

Among other reasons, that's why in business to grow is not necessarily the same as to generate EV.

Point 2: Economic value is not only extrinsic economic value.

Any extrinsic EV is just a price paid in a market. Only if you believe that any price always reflects a reasonable and fair valuation can you affirm that extrinsic EV is the only EV that matters.

Experience tells us that this is not normally the case. In fact, financial bubbles do exist. And, as the old proverb says, wisdom begins with calling things by their right names.

Point 3: Economic value is a matter of generating positive total cash flows.

Cash flows mean real money, not just accounting profits or margins. And total cash flows mean real money coming from all the operational aspects of the business, not only from the day-to-day operations reflected in the income statement. In order to generate EV, any company has to manage not only based on the information coming from the income statement, but also from the statement reflected in the operational assets.

That is why we use free cash flow (FCF), which is the balance of cash in/cash out associated with the operational aspects of the business.

Point 4: Free cash flows must be relevant.

This is especially important in digital business. Not any type of FCF is relevant to measure the EV associated with a management decision. They have to be differential (because of the management decisions taken) and sustainable in time (net of the reaction of competitors).

In digital business, it's relatively frequent to justify an investment because of the new users that arise from the decision. But these new users will only generate EV if:

1. They are really new and differential users for the business.
2. They will generate positive and differential FCF for the business.
3. They will generate sustainable FCF for the business.

Note what this means:

1. We have to consider only differential, new, incremental users that come from the decision. Shared users are not differential, unless we can offer

them new services and generate new cash flows because of the management decision.

2. These incremental users have to generate sustainable cash flows, which mean that they will remain in the company for ever, no matter the action of the competition. In other words, any differential and sustainable cash flow is net from the action of the competition. Note that this net cash flow is not always negative, as noted in previous chapters.

A similar analysis has to be done for the expected cash flows associated with synergies:

1. Be sure they are positive (or that you are not missing the negatives).
2. Be sure they are differential.
3. Be sure they are sustainable in time.

Point 5: Monetization of users

To positively monetize new users, they have to be differential, sustainable and generate positive cash flows. Note that, in some cases, monetization from new users can be negative, as far as the expected synergies associated with some decisions become negative.

Point 6: Financing matters.

We already know that FCFs must be positive, differential and sustainable. But FCFs also have to be enough to make a decision economically feasible and profitable. In other words, financing for a given FCF does not always make the decision feasible and equally profitable.

This is a point easily forgotten. Economic feasibility and economic profitability depend not only on the generated FCFs, but also on the way in which we finance our decisions. For example, if Microsoft decides to buy LinkedIn by paying $26.3 billion for the company, the expected EV that this decision will generate for the present shareholders of Microsoft depends not only on the future differential FCFs, but also on the way in which Microsoft decides to finance this operation.

Point 6: Risk matters

An important part of EV involves the consideration of the risks associated with corporate decision-making that targets the creation of value. In this sense, going too far is just as bad as coming up short.

Where are the risks in our valuation model that uses cash flows discounted at weighted average cost of capital (WACC)?

In FCFs, one must consider the main operating risks inherent in the different business policies of the company involving, for example, sales, personnel, logistics, production, overheads, collection and investment. Once these risks have been identified and their importance quantified, they are normally included in the valuation model through sensitivity analyses or probability simulations.

WACC includes financial risk stemming from the financial leverage ratio implied by the capital structure; risks perceived by shareholders, which form part of the cost of equity (market-risk premium and systematic operating and financial risks of the company); and risks perceived by financial entities that are included in the cost of debt.

Point 7: Extrinsic value versus intrinsic value

As noted earlier, extrinsic (market-based) and intrinsic (business model-based) approaches are complementary, and give a (hopefully) reasonable opinion about EV.

Common sense tells us that long term everyone will pay more for a company if that it will likely produce better returns. Nobody invests his/her money to lose it. So, from an investor perspective, any extrinsic value should be explained in terms of its associated FCF estimated in present value.

For mature and relatively low capital intensive industries, the operational earnings of a company can be considered a good proxy to its FCF. Since FCF has three components, assuming the operational working capital (OWC) component is close to zero, and that the company needs capital expenditure equal to the depreciation and amortization expenses, then FCF can be considered very close to the earnings before interest and after taxes (EBIaT), a typical measure of net (after taxes) operational earnings (without interest expenses).

In these cases, the expected generation of EBIaT of the company is a good proxy of the expected generation of FCF, and any comparison of EV/EBIaT can be easily related to the needed FCF to justify the valuation.

When the company operates in a neither mature nor low capital intensive industry, we have to consider the investments in OWC and capital expenditure that any business needs to survive. This is the case for most digital businesses.

Point 8: Value proposition versus value perception

Extrinsic and intrinsic value meet when the value proposition communicated for the company matches the expected value perceived for the market. This is an important point to be considered, especially for public companies where investors' relations departments have become a crucial element in building up credibility and ensuring sustainability.

In fact, any value-based management orientation has to identify the eventual gap between the value associated to the current business model and the value expected from the market. When a gap exists, the company has to develop the actions needed to cover this gap.

Point 9: What about metrics?

It's obvious that there are some advantages in using only a simple metric (number of users, for example) to justify an investment decision. Among others, it's simple, clear and understandable. And, providing the market is signaling a reasonable EV, it gives a useful price.

The problem is that the extrinsic EV is not always reasonable and, consequently, it's very convenient to understand it in terms of the implicit assumptions about the key value drivers that are associated with its intrinsic EV, as explained above.

Additionally, to create economic value we have to select the right alternative but we also have to implement it. And this implementation can become impossible when the people responsible for it do not fully understand the underlying assumptions implicit in the expected EV to be created, or when these assumptions are not realistic and/or reasonable.

Keeping these comments in mind, we can conclude that any value metric is a shortcut to analyze EV, and it can be very useful in communicating and setting up management objectives in the implementation of any value-based management approach.

In any case, the key point is not which value metric we use (digital oriented or not), but whether its quantification is consistent with the general objective about EV creation.

In summary, regarding the relationship between value metrics and the measure of EV, we can establish the following conclusions:

1. Most of the metrics do not measure correctly the value created by a business decision, as they refer to data for just one year, while business decisions create value over the whole period in which they take place.
2. When they are used as a measure of value created by the management of a company, it is necessary to bear in mind the conceptual limitations inherent in their formulation.
3. It is therefore necessary to know what a metric measures and to act accordingly.
4. The use of any value metric must be linked to business value generators, as a relative rather than absolute formulation that facilitates the achievement of partial objectives related to a general objective.

A Framework to Analyze Economic Value

Summarizing some of the ideas developed in this book, in Table 6.1 we propose a practical framework to analyze the EV associated with a management decision in a digital economy.

Following this framework, we can now review whether or not the expected EV associated with some of the examples already discussed in this book is reasonable.

Revisiting Some Examples

Facebook and WhatsApp

Table 6.2 shows how to apply the framework to this particular case.

From the information summarized in Table 6.1, we can draw similar conclusions to those derived in Chapter 3:

1. The price of $19,000 million for the equity seems excessive.
2. This price will only be justified if Facebook (FB) is able to monetize the new users acquired with WhatsApp (WHP).

Table 6.1 A two-step framework to analyze economic value

Step 1: Focus valuation	
Value of what	
Value for what	
Value for whom	
Value in what circumstances	
Step 2: Analyze the valuation	
2.1. Extrinsic value	
Listed companies:	Premium paid
Private companies	EV/EBITDA
	E/EBITDA
2.2. Intrinsic value through DCF	
Announced synergies	Differential, sustainable, positive
Reasonable evolution of FCF	Evolution from negative to positive
Key: TV	Needed growth rate
Changes in WACC	Reasonable capital structure
2.3. Intrinsic value through real options	
Define the statistical behavior of the underlying asset.	
Needed volatility of the underlying asset to explain the price	

Table 6.2 WhatsApp acquisition by Facebook in 2014

Step 1: Focus valuation	
Value of what	**WhatsApp**
Value for what	**To be acquired by Facebook**
Value for whom	**From the perspective of Facebook's shareholders**
Value in what circumstances	**In March 2014**
Step 2: Analyze the valuation	
2.1. Extrinsic value	
Listed companies: Premium paid	**N/A**
Private Companies: EV/users	**$42.4 per user**
EV/revenue	**47.7 times**
2.2. Intrinsic Value through DCF	
Announced synergies	**None**
Reasonable evolution of FCF	**From 500 to 1,000 in five years**
Key: TV	**Needed g of 4.7%**
Changes in WACC	**No debt. WACC at 8%**
2.3. Intrinsic value through real options	
Define the statistical behavior of the underlying asset	**Normal distribution**
Needed volatility of underlying asset to justify price	**Higher than 100%**

3. One way to do this is to assume that:

   a. Differential revenues will grow at an accumulated average annual rate of 123.4% in the next five years.
   b. From that moment on, WHP will be able to grow at more than 5%, keeping its profitability forever, without new investments in OWC and in capital expenditure.

4. In any case, the acquisition was financed partially with new FB shares. In the accepted exchange rate between shares of FB and shares of WHP, there seems to be an excessive level of dilution for the old shareholders of FB.

5. Financed only with equity, the economic profitability for the shareholders is 14.4%. This profitability would have been higher if the acquisition had also been financed with debt. For example, financed with a capital structure of 30% of debt, the economic profitability for the shareholders would have been 19.2%.

6. Complementary to this, we can quantify this expected monetization of users by assuming that, with the acquisition of WHP, FB is buying a put option on the shares of WHP. According to some reasonable assumptions in line with the valuation made through discounted cash flow (DCF), the price of $19,000 million needs a final price for WHP above $46.6 billion.

Table 6.3 Instagram acquisition by Facebook in 2012

Step 1: Focus valuation	
Value of what	**Instagram**
Value for what	**To be acquired by Facebook**
Value for whom	**From the perspective of Facebook's shareholders**
Value in what circumstances	**In April 2012**
Step 2: Analyze the valuation	
2.1. Extrinsic value	
Listed companies: Premium paid	**N/A**
Private Companies: EV/users	**$33 per user**
EV/revenue	**N/A**
2.2. Intrinsic value through DCF	
Announced synergies	**None**
Reasonable evolution of FCF	**From 214 and growing at 4% next four years**
Key: TV	**Needed growth rate of 3%**
Changes in WACC	**No changes. WACC at 10%**
2.3. Intrinsic Value through Real Options	
Define the statistical behavior of the underlying asset	**Normal distribution**
Needed volatility of underlying asset to justify price	**Lower than 50%**

Facebook and Instagram

Table 6.3 includes key information about the acquisition of Instagram (IG) by FB in 2012.

If we compare Table 6.2 with Table 6.3, it is clear that Facebook paid a more reasonable price for IG than for WHP. Why? Because in the case of IG, we can apply more reasonable assumptions to gain an intrinsic EV of the company that is similar to the price paid (see Table 6.4).

More specifically, to justify the price paid for WHP we would need a terminal value (TV) with a growth rate of 4.7%, while in the case of IG the growth rate is only 3%. Additionally, using a real option approach to justify the EV, the volatility of the underlying asset in the case of WHP needs to be higher than 100%, while in IG it is lower than 50%.

IBM and Truven Health Analytics

In mid-February 2016, IBM announced the acquisition of Truven Health Analytics Inc. (THA) for $2.6 billion, in a bid to expand its already

Table 6.4 Comparing two acquisitions

Facebook's acquisition			Instagram's acquisition		
Step 2: Analyze the valuation			**Step 2: Analyze the valuation**		
2.1. Extrinsic value			2.1. Extrinsic value		
Listed companies: Premium paid	N/A		Listed companies: Premium p	N/A	
Private companies: EV/users	$42.4 per user		Private companies: EV/users	$33 per user	
EV/revenue	47.7 times		EV/revenue	N/A	
2.2. Intrinsic value through DCF			2.2. Intrinsic value through DCF		
Announced synergies	None		Announced synergies	None	
Reasonable evolution of FCF	From 500 to 1,000 in five years		Reasonable evolution of FCF	From 214 and growing at 4% next four years	
Key: TV	Needed growth rate of 4.7%		Key: TV	Needed growth rate of 3%	
Changes in WACC	No debt. WACC at 8%		Changes in WACC	No changes. WACC at 10%	
2.3. Intrinsic value through real options			2.3. Intrinsic value through real options		
Define the statistical behavior of the underlying asset	Normal distribution		Define the statistical behavior of the underlying asset	Normal distribution	
Needed volatility of underlying asset to justify price	Higher than 100%		Needed volatility of underlying asset to justify price	Lower than 50%	

Table 6.5 THA's acquisition by IBM in 2016

Step 1: Focus valuation	
Value of what	Truven Health Analytics
Value for what	To be acquired by IBM
Value for whom	From the perspective of IBM's shareholders
Value in what circumstances	In February 2016
Step 2: Analyze the valuation	
2.1. Extrinsic value	
Listed companies: Premium paid	**N/A**
Private Companies: EV/EBITDA	**20 times**
2.2. Intrinsic value through DCF	
Announced synergies	**None**
Reasonable evolution of FCF	**FCF goes from 10 to 100 in five years**
Key: TV	**Needed growth rate of 7.63%**
Changes in WACC	**No changes. WACC at 10%**
2.3. Intrinsic value through real options	
Define the statistical behavior of the underlying asset	**Normal distribution**
Needed volatility of underlying asset to justify price	**Higher than 100%**

considerable presence in the health-care industry. THA supplies health-care data services to employers, hospitals and drug makers to help them gauge the efficacy of products and services.

Once more, THA's acquisition by IBM was considered to be a reasonable strategic movement which makes a lot of sense. As always, the question mark was not over the operation, but over the price. Was IBM overvaluing THA when it paid $2.6 billion for the company? How can we evaluate an intangible asset such as data?

If we apply the proposed framework to this case, we get the information summarized in Table 6.5.

According to data included in Table 6.3, the price of $2.6 billion looks excessive: to justify this, THA would need a TV with a perpetual growth rate of 7.63%. Additionally, using a real option approach to justify the EV, the volatility of the underlying asset needs to be higher than 100%.

Evaluating Twitter

At the end of 2015 the market capitalization of Twitter was $17,500 million. Since the amount of debt was $1,602 million, the market value of Twitter was $19,102 million.

Table 6.6 Market valuation of Twitter in 2016

Step 1: Focus valuation	
Value of what	**Twitter**
Value for what	**In relation to the market value**
Value for whom	**From the perspective of an eventual investor in Twitter**
Value in what circumstances	**Beginning 2016**
Step 2: Analyze the valuation	
2.1. Extrinsic value	
Listed companies: Premium paid	**N/A**
Private companies: EV/EBITDA	**N/A (Twitter has losses)**
2.2. Intrinsic value through DCF	
Announced synergies	**None**
Reasonable evolution of FCF	**Change to positive FCF of $91 millions. Growth of 33% in eight years**
Key: TV	**Needed growth rate of 5.68%**
Changes in WACC	**No changes. WACC at 8%**
2.3. Intrinsic value through real options	
Define the statistical behavior of the underlying asset	**Normal distribution**
Needed volatility of underlying asset to justify price	**Higher than 100%**

Does this market value make sense? Is it based on a reasonable intrinsic valuation? If so, in what terms?

Table 6.6 summarizes some key information about Twitter's valuation at the beginning of 2016.

According to this information, to justify Twitter's valuation we have to consider:

1. The main question mark hanging over the future of Twitter is whether the company will be able to monetize the services provided to its users. So far, Twitter has been unable to do this, consistently showing losses and generating negative cash flow.
2. At the end of 2015 the market capitalization of Twitter was $17,500 million. Since the amount of debt was $1,602 million, the market value of Twitter was $19,102 million.
3. To analyze how reasonable this EV is we have to justify the required evolution of the expected FCFs and TV.

4. In terms of FCF, Twitter will need:

   a. To increase the number of users from 310 million to 2,282 million in eight years, if the company keeps the ratio FCF/user. This means an accumulative yearly growth rate (AYGR) of 33%.
   b. To increase the ratio FCF/user from $0.29 million to $0.86 million in eight years, if the company sees an AYGR in the number of users of 14%.
   c. To increase the time each user spends daily on the website from 20 minutes to 147 minutes, if the company keeps constant the ratio of average daily FCF per minute spent.
   d. To increase the average daily FCF per minute spent from $12,470 to $91,770, if the company maintains the time spent daily per user at a constant level.

5. In terms of TV, Twitter must have a final value of 26.8 times its last earnings before interest, taxes, depreciation and amortization (EBITDA). This is equivalent to the value of its last FCF growing at an annual rate of 5.68% forever.

Searching for Reasonable Value

By using this two-step framework to measure the expected EV associated with any management decision we can analyze how reasonable any valuation is.

In Table 6.7 we have summarized some points which help to identify what we believe is a reasonable valuation in digital assets.

In practical terms, to reach a reasonable valuation we should consider the following points:

1. For extrinsic valuation, judge the price paid in relation to the price of similar transactions.
2. Estimate the sustainability of the market price based on a reasonable intrinsic valuation.
3. For intrinsic valuations, be careful with TVs which imply a rate of perpetual growth higher than the expected inflation in nominal terms.
4. Look for specific measures and actions to implement the expected synergies.
5. Do not undervalue competition's answer to your value proposal.
6. Do not underestimate associated costs for implementing expected synergies.

Table 6.7 Identifying a reasonable valuation

Key elements to analyze a valuation		
How to identify a reasonable valuation		
1. Extrinsic value		
	Measure	Reasonable answers
Listed companies:	Premium paid	In line with market. Not higher
Private companies	EV/EBITDA	In line with market. Not higher
	E/EBITDA	In line with market. Not higher
2. 1. Intrinsic Value through DCF		
Announced synergies	Differential, sustainable, positive	See specific measures to implement them
Reasonable evolution of FCF	Evolution from negative to positive	See sustainability of changes
Key: TV	Needed growth rate	Not higher than 3%, in perpetuity
Changes in WACC	Capital structure	Not changes higher than 10%
2.2. Intrinsic value through real options		
Needed volatility of the underlying asset		Not higher than 40–50%

7. Adjust your offered acquisition's price to a conservative expected future, never to an optimistic one.
8. Any valuation based on real options should be consistent with the valuation based on a discounted cash flow approach.

Let us apply this approach to understand a negotiation about price in a recent acquisition.

On May 23, 2016 Bayer made an offer to buy 100% of Monsanto's equity, at a price of $122 per share. This price implied a valuation of Monsanto's equity of $62 billion, to be paid in cash, with a premium of 36% of market price.

On May 25, 2016 Monsanto's Board of Directors declined the offer, considering that the price was low. In their opinion, a more accurate price for Monsanto would be $140 per share.

How can we analyze whether the offered price was reasonable?

If we use our two-steps approach to extrinsic and intrinsic value, we get the information summarized in Table 6.8.

Table 6.8 Valuation of Monsanto

Valuation of Monsanto in the context of an eventual acquisition from Bayer May 2016		
Key elements to analyze a valuation		
1. Extrinsic value		
Listed companies:	Premium offered	36%
Private companies	EV/EBITDA	15.34
	Goodwill/FCF	27.50
2. Intrinsic value through DCF		
Announced synergies	Differential, sustainable, positive	$1,500 million in three years
Reasonable evolution of FCF	Evolution from negative to positive	A sustainable FCF per year of $2,000 million growing at 5%
Key: TV	Needed g	lower than 2%
Changes in WACC	Capital structure	60E/40D
3. Intrinsic value through real options		
Needed volatility of the underlying asset		lower than 20%

According to extrinsic values, the offer of $122 per share looks very attractive, since the market price at that time was around $90 per share. It also looks very convenient in terms of comparable, the offer is also very convenient, with a significant ratio EV/EBITDA.

But what is good value in relative terms does not always remain good value in terms of fundamentals. And this is one of these cases.

Assuming that Monsanto will keep a sustainable FCF of $2,000 million, growing at 5% for the next five years, and that it will have the expected synergies of $500 million in the next three years, we need a TV with a growth rate lower than 2% to reach an EV that is in line with the offered price.

Clearly, there is room for negotiation in terms of intrinsic value.

As we know, in mid-July 2016 Bayer made a new offer of $125 per share. This offer was not accepted by Monsanto's Board of Directors.

Finally, in mid-September 2016 Bayer announced an agreement with Monsanto to buy the company at a price of $128 per share.

Summary

1. Summarizing some of the ideas developed in this book, in this chapter we propose a practical framework to analyze the EV associated with management decisions about digital assets.
2. By using this two-steps framework to measure the expected EV associated with any management decision we can analyze how reasonable any valuation is.
3. In practical terms, to reach a reasonable valuation we should consider the following points:

   a. For extrinsic valuation, judge the price paid in relation to the price of similar transactions.
   b. Estimate the sustainability of the market price based on a reasonable intrinsic valuation.
   c. For intrinsic valuations, be careful with TVs which imply a rate of perpetual growth higher than the expected inflation in nominal terms.
   d. Look for specific measures and actions to implement the expected synergies.
   e. Do not undervalue competition's answer to your value proposal.
   f. Do not underestimate associated costs to implement expected synergies.
   g. Adjust your offered acquisition's price to a conservative expected future, never to an optimistic one.
   h. Any valuation based on real options should be consistent with the valuation based on a discounted cash flow approach.

7

Summary and Conclusions

Chapter 1

1. Digital technologies are reshaping our individual, social and cultural lives in historically unprecedented ways. The integration of digital technologies into everyday life has a range of consequences for individuals, families, communities, governments and organizations.
2. This digital revolution, known as the Third Industrial Revolution, is the change from analogue, mechanical and electronic technology to digital technology.
3. Customers are quickly adopting new channels – including web, social and mobile – and want to use them to contact the companies with whom they do business.
4. To meet the high expectations of their consumers, companies have started to accelerate the digitization of their business processes. One of the most salient aspects of the digital revolution is e-commerce.
5. The digital economy refers to an economy that is based on digital technologies, although we increasingly perceive this as conducting business through markets based on the Internet and the World Wide Web.
6. Typically, Internet business models are categorized as business-to-consumer (B2C), business-to-business (B2B) and more recently consumer-to-consumer (C2C).
7. B2C and B2B models typically sell goods and services or provide information designed to help visitors make purchase decisions. C2C models involve consumer-to-consumer information or product exchange.

© The Author(s) 2017
F.J. López Lubián, J. Esteves, *Value in a Digital World*,
DOI 10.1007/978-3-319-51750-6_7

8. In the most basic sense, a business model is the method of doing business by which a company can sustain itself – that is, generate revenue. Based on the revenue model perspective, we can define a taxonomy of the main web business models, identifying nine different types.

9. It should come as no surprise that the continuing development of the Internet consistently results in significant shifts as to how businesses operate, how consumers react and how products are bought and sold. Naturally, the very fundamental structures of business models continue to evolve in line with this, becoming far more flexible and innovative than has ever been seen before. An example of this is the emergence of the digital sharing economy.

Chapter 2

1. Economic value (EV) is not just a qualitative value, as, for example, sentimental value is. A house may have considerable sentimental value but a very low EV.

2. EV is not just an accounting value. A company may have a relevant accounting value but a not so brilliant EV. Why? Because the accounting value deals with historical information, presented in an accurate, systematic and consistent way, and for the EV we also have to consider the expected future and the associated risks.

3. Any measure of EV must include an appropriate conceptual and practical response to three elements: the generation of real money (cash flows); the expected future of the business; the associated risks.

4. There are two ways to measure EV.

5. First, we have the extrinsic EV, which is an EV that comes from what the market considers. Extrinsic EV is certainly a reference to be considered, but it's not always the best way to get a reasonable EV.

6. That's why we have to complement the extrinsic EV with the intrinsic EV. For the intrinsic EV we try to calculate the EV of something based on its accounting value and its future business plans. In other words, we do not take it for granted that the price will naturally reflect this transition from accounting value to a reasonable EV.

7. To create EV in a digital business, and in any business for that matter, we have to generate high enough differential and sustainable cash flows, so that when discounted at the minimum expected economic profitability

desired by our providers of financial resources (debt and equity), the present value would still be positive and better than the alternatives.

8. In digital business, it is relatively usual to justify an investment because of the new users resulting from the decision.

9. Before paying for new users, we have to understand how the business model of the digital company is able to generate revenue and make money through these customers.

10. We have to realize that this means considering only differential, new, incremental users who result from the decision. Shared users are not differential, unless we can offer them new services and generate new cash flows because of the decision.

11. These incremental users have to generate sustainable cash flows, which means that these users will remain in the company for ever, regardless the actions of the competition.

12. In practical terms, this means that we should consider only users who are incremental and active. Registered and passive users are good, but not good enough.

13. How a management decision is financed can affect the expected EV of that decision and the distribution of that EV.

14. To cope with the digital revolution, innovation is needed more than ever. Companies need to constantly innovate to keep pace with ever-changing consumer demand.

15. New product and service innovations can be categorized in three levels of innovation: Sustaining, Breakthrough and Radical.

16. The higher the importance of innovation to become a survivor, the higher the importance of operational flexibility to create economic value. We can introduce the value of this operational flexibility in our traditional DCF approach in different ways: probabilistic sensitivity analysis; transforming some of the variables from deterministic to probabilistic, and estimating a probabilistic economic value based on simulations; and introducing the economic value of some real options associated to the business model.

17. Any value metric is a shortcut to analyse economic value and it can be very useful to establish and communicate management objectives for the implementation of any value-based management approach.

18. In any case, the key point is not what value metric we use (digital oriented or not), but whether the quantification of that value metric is consistent with the more general objective of economic value creation.

Chapter 3

1. When we evaluate a company we want to have a reasonable answer to the question of how much we should pay for that company, considering its EV. This means that any valuation is an opinion and, like any opinion, it can be a very reasonable judgment or complete nonsense.
2. To get a reasonable valuation we need to focus that valuation. To do this we have to clarify issues such as what we want to evaluate in a company; for what purpose we want to evaluate a company; from what perspective we want to evaluate a company; under what circumstances we want to evaluate a company.
3. Contrary to common belief, relative (extrinsic) and fundamental (intrinsic) values are not incompatible, and are actually complementary. The difference between the two should serve to show the EV of a control participation in the company.
4. To establish a reasonable price using the relative value it is important to make sure that the markets on which the comparison is based are comparable.
5. To obtain a reasonable price using the intrinsic value it is essential to understand the valuation model used, the business being valued and how they adapt to each other.
6. In order to obtain the correct ratio between price and value it is essential to consider what is being bought and how it is being bought. For example, buying a controlling interest in a public company is not the same as buying a non-controlling interest in a private company.
7. Once the value of the company has been made based on an open scenario, the process should be rounded off by examining real factors, such as possible limitations to the distribution of cash flows among those supplying the funds (capital and liabilities).
8. These adjustments are particularly important when valuing mergers and acquisitions transactions in a multinational context, and must include an analysis of possible fiscal differences resulting from different rates of taxation between countries, the financing of the foreign company by the parent company once it has been acquired and the alternatives available for repatriation of monetary flows to investors through various dividend share-out mechanisms.
9. These valuation principles can be applied to any business transaction in order to understand the impact of key value drivers on the final price and how reasonable the assumptions are that are used to reach that price.

10. In transactions dealing with the digital world, it is common to justify prices based on the number of users. By applying these concepts about EV we can better understand the implicit assumptions needed to make possible the monetization of these new users.

Chapter 4

1. For any extrinsic valuation, try to understand the influence of short-term (speculative) movements on market value.
2. Decide the type of investor you want to be: short term, speculative; long term, looking for sustainable value.
3. Estimate the sustainability of the market price based on a reasonable intrinsic valuation.
4. Select a key value driver (KVD) and determine how reasonable the assumptions are that you need on this KVD in order to obtain the present market value.
5. Be aware of the type of share you are buying, in terms of liquidity, control and rights.
6. Be sure that complementary business will offer real synergies. Consider both positive and negative synergies.
7. Identify actions that are needed to bring those synergies about. Quantify their economic impact.
8. Don't undervalue competition's answer to your value proposal.
9. Don't underestimate associated costs for implementing expected synergies.
10. Adjust your offered acquisition's price to a conservative expected future, never to an optimistic one.

Chapter 5

1. For any company, to deliver EV for its stakeholders it's not only a matter of delivering accounting value or accounting profitability. In that sense, it would be incorrect to believe that only accounting metrics, such as return on assets or return on equity, measure the EV.

2. For any company, delivering EV for its stakeholders is a matter of generating differential and sustainable free cash flow (FCF), and in an amount that covers their expected return.
3. If a company has problems in generating this required FCF, the solution is not to increase the total FCF by decreasing the FCF required by the operational stakeholders. The solution should be to implement changes (if possible) to better manage all the operational policies of the company in order to increase the generation of FCF.
4. The erosion effect has to be considered, and in some cases this effect can be positive in terms of differential FCF. This tends to be the case with digital business, where innovation and competition are key factors to create EV.
5. Experiences of the implementation of digitization processes are not always positive. Among other reasons this is because, for any company, becoming digital has to be linked to its strategy and business sustainability.
6. In order to avoid pitfalls, it's important to distinguish between digitization and digital transformation.
7. Digitization is about digitizing processes, services and products. A typical digitization might offer new services via apps.
8. Digital transformation is about integrating three main components: products/services, customers and business model. It's about creating a new business model which reaches new customers, offers new services and products, and generates differential new profits.
9. New trends in the digital world include big data, artificial intelligence, robotics, the Internet of Things and augmented and virtual reality.

Chapter 6

1. Summarizing some of the ideas developed in this book, in this chapter we propose a practical methodology to analyze the EV associated with management decisions about digital assets.
2. By using this two-steps methodology to measure the expected EV associated with any management decision we can analyze how reasonable any valuation is.
3. In practical terms, to reach a reasonable valuation we should consider the following points:

(a) For extrinsic valuation, judge the price paid in relation to the price of similar transactions.
(b) Estimate the sustainability of the market price based on a reasonable intrinsic valuation.
(c) For intrinsic valuations, be careful with terminal values which imply a rate of perpetual growth higher than expected inflation in nominal terms.
(d) Look for specific measures and actions to implement the expected synergies.
(e) Do not undervalue competition's answer to your value proposal.
(f) Do not underestimate the associated costs to implement expected synergies.
(g) Adjust your offered acquisition's price to a conservative expected future, never to an optimistic one.
(h) Any valuation based on real options should be consistent with the valuation based on a discounted cash flow approach.

Index

© The Author(s) 2017
F.J. López Lubián, J. Esteves, *Value in a Digital World*,
DOI 10.1007/978-3-319-51750-6_7

The manufacturer's authorised representative in the EU is Springer
Nature Customer Service Centre GmbH, Europaplatz 3, 69115 Heidelberg,
Germany. If you have any concerns regarding our products, please
contact ProductSafety@springernature.com

Printed and bound by CPI Group (UK) Ltd, Croydon, CR0 4YY
27/04/2026
02097625-0003